Jean-François Caron

The Moral Dilemmas of Fighting Terrorism and Guerrilla Groups

Facing Contemporary Terrorism

—

Edited by
Jean-François Caron

Volume 2

Jean-François Caron

The Moral Dilemmas of Fighting Terrorism and Guerrilla Groups

—

DE GRUYTER

ISBN 978-3-11-162166-1
e-ISBN (PDF) 978-3-11-075756-9
e-ISBN (EPUB) 978-3-11-075758-3
ISSN 2749-1188
e-ISSN 2749-1196

Library of Congress Control Number: 2022946317

Bibliographic information published by the Deutsche Nationalbibliothek
The Deutsche Nationalbibliothek lists this publication in the Deutsche Nationalbibliografie;
detailed bibliographic data are available on the internet at http://dnb.dnb.de.

© 2024 Walter de Gruyter GmbH, Berlin/Boston
This volume is text- and page-identical with the hardback published in 2023.
Cover image: Lorado / iStock / Getty Images Plus

www.degruyter.com

Contents

Introduction

Most of us living in the West became acquainted with the reality of terrorism as a clear and present danger only in the last 20 years after the 9/11 attacks triggered numerous attacks against civilians by individuals who had pledged allegiance to Al Qaeda or the Islamic State of Iraq and the Levant (ISIL). In this regard, we can think of the 2004 attacks in Madrid's commuter train system in which 193 people died and around 2,000 were injured; or similar attacks that took place one year later in London's public transport system that killed 56 people and injured another 784 and the 2015 Paris attacks that killed and injured 130 and 416 innocent people, respectively.

However, it would be a mistake to conclude that terrorism is a contemporary phenomenon. As highlighted by the most famous analyst of this type of political violence, Walter Laqueur, if we are to think of terrorism as distinct from regular warfare (which is a mistake, but more on this later), attacks by small groups of irregular fighters against state actors or civilians go back to time immemorial (Laqueur & Wall, 2018, p. 27). As amazing as it sounds, it must be stressed that despite its longevity and the fact that it has been widely discussed, terrorism remains a widely misunderstood reality. The fact that the international community still does not agree on a common definition of terrorism is probably the most obvious testimony in this regard. The primary objective of this book is to shed some light on the nature of terrorism by explaining how distinctive it is from another well-known form of irregular warfare that it is too often confounded with, namely guerrilla.

Terrorism is usually associated with barbaric entities that have no consideration for innocent people's lives and whose actions are often thought to be irrational and commanded by divinity. Guerrilla warfare is, for its part, linked with groups that have more noble aims, such as those fighting for national liberation. As proof of this distinctive manner of assessing these two forms of political violence, many individuals who led and were involved in the latter form of warfare are now celebrated as heroes in many societies[1], while terrorists do not share the same historical fate (for a reason that is far from being a subjective matter, as I will discuss in this book). However, although tempting and rather common in people's viewpoint, this manner of distinguishing terrorism from guerrilla by focusing on the irrationality of the former and the noble character of the latter

---

[1] In this regard, we can refer to Michael Collins who played a pivotal role in the creation of the Irish Republic and was positively depicted in the 1996 award-winning biographical movie, in which he was personified by actor Liam Neeson.

https://doi.org/10.1515/9783110757569-001

is highly problematic. Indeed, history has proven that the resort to terrorist tactics has sometimes been the result of a well-thought rational decision by groups that were also fighting for their national liberation, while many groups animated by religious beliefs refused to resort to this type of violence. In return, terrorism was also a privileged tactic of non-religious groups, which makes the use of rational/irrational, barbaric/noble aims, and religious/non-religious dichotomies inappropriate tools in defining and distinguishing between these two types of violence.

Another mistake would be to limit terrorism as an inherent tactic of non-state actors. There is a common misconception in this regard which is largely the result of the double standards used by states that have given themselves the monopoly over legitimate violence as a mean to always find noble ways of justifying their resort to war in opposition to non-state entities often presented as rogue, criminal, and immoral in their aims and means of action. Additionally, we should not forget that from an etymological perspective the word terrorism derives from the French word '*terreur*' which was a clearly affirmed political tactic used by French revolutionaries like Robespierre or Saint-Just, thus making it a form of violence that is not solely restricted to non-state actors[2]. Furthermore, in the past, even contemporary democratic states have explicitly chosen to resort to indiscriminate tactics that aimed at terrorising their enemies, as was the case with Winston Churchill's order to his Air Command to bomb German cities during WWII. Consequently, these common misconceptions call for a better assessment of the uniqueness of terrorism and guerrilla warfare.

With these clarifications, it will be easier to understand the inherent immorality of terrorism and how it differs from guerrilla warfare. Thus, the apparent moral superiority of the latter over the former should not necessarily lead us to conclude that resorting to guerrilla as a form of violence is always morally acceptable. In contrast, if the act of killing can sometimes be justified in this type of warfare, this can only be a last-resort option and only when the situation has reached a certain extreme. As a result, the co-called superiority of guerrilla over terrorism does not give *carte blanche* to the former when it comes to violent actions. This type of violence also comes with its own string of moral questions that cannot be ignored. The first two chapters will focus on the distinction between terrorism and guerrilla warfare as well as the moral limits of the latter.

Additionally, although it may look like a straightforward affair between good and absolute evil, the war against terror is more complex and brings in its wake many ethical dilemmas, that is, a confrontation between two moral categorical

---

2 In its peak period, *la terreur* led to the execution of around 40,000 people in a single month.

imperatives in which respect for one will inevitably lead to violation of the other. As argued elsewhere (Caron, 2014), battlefield mercy killing is probably the best example of such a clash between two moral norms. Indeed, in these situations, soldiers are forced to choose, on the one hand, to abide by the moral obligation not to kill a vulnerable human being; and on the other hand, not to let this individual endure the terrible suffering resulting from what appears to be a lethal wound. In such situations, whatever the decision taken by soldiers confronted by this dilemma will be, the outcome will necessarily be morally questioned by some who will come to believe that the other alternative should have prevailed. Unfortunately, when it comes to these categorical moral imperatives, people who are facing them are caught in a "catch-22" as it is impossible to hierarchise them and reach an agreement that one decision is better than the other based on a rational assessment of the situation.

In the case of terrorism, I see three dilemmas of this sort that are appearing to be opposed to states' obligations to protect the lives of their citizens. First, it is the responsibility of states to protect the lives of their citizens that are directly threatened by terrorist organizations. Abiding by this obligation therefore calls for action on their part. In return, as is evident from Afghanistan and Iraq, fighting terrorism seems to come at the expense of a disproportionate number of civilians' lives abroad. This has led authors to argue that Western states simply transfer the risk from their own civilians to those who have the misfortune of living in countries or areas where terrorists are operating. Consequently, this 'risk transfer' is highly problematic from a moral perspective (as well as from a political perspective as these military interventions were unable to even eradicate the terrorist threats they were promising to achieve) which seems to be creating a situation where states fighting this sort of threat are condemned to violate a moral imperative no matter what they decide to do: either wait and let their civilians be killed first by terrorists or transfer that risk to civilians abroad as if 'their lives' are less important than 'our lives'.

Second, the status of captured terrorists raises a similar dilemma. Again, for the sake of respecting their obligation to protect the lives of their civilians, are states allowed to use methods of torture against captured terrorists who may possess sensitive information about upcoming attacks? It is not surprising that torture is an endemic reality in many authoritarian and totalitarian states, but the 9/11 attacks have also led Liberal states to engage in what has been labelled as 'enhanced interrogation techniques': a euphemism that poorly hides the fact that these methods are nothing less than torture. However, the resort to these techniques has often been justified through the lens of a 'ticking bomb scenario', that is, when a state is facing a terrorist threat that cannot be prevented in a conventional and lawful manner. The ethical dilemma here is the choice between doing everything to prevent civilians from being killed or respecting the non-combatant status of a captured terrorist. If the former categorical imperative is privileged, this means that someone who has regained immunity against harm will nonetheless be physically harmed, whereas abiding by the latter deontological rule may result in a violation of a state's duty to protect its people from harm.

Lastly, if we are thinking of war as the continuation of politics through other means, it remains that the return to politics ought to be the primary objective of statesmen, meaning that finding ways to end this form of violence constitutes a moral necessity. There are several reasons behind this, but the most obvious is that despite states' best intentions, war always brings chaos, destruction, and death to those who should not be impacted, namely, civilians. Precisely, it has been estimated that the ratio of civilians for every combatant killed was two to one during the Korean and Vietnam War, three to one in Afghanistan, four to one in Iraq and in Kosovo, up to five to one during the 1982 Lebanon war and a staggering ten to one in Chechnya. Considering this goal, the question is whether the deliberate targeting of civilians might be excused to end a conflict. More specifically, can terrorism (as I will argue in this book, the deliberate targeting of civilians truly defines this type of violence) ever be justified? This interrogation clearly shows the ethical dilemma between states' moral obligation to protect civilians during wartime and the need for peace which can be viewed as a primary good. Similarly, to the previously mentioned case of battlefield mercy killing, choosing one option over the other will inevitably lead individuals who are expected to make a decision to violate a moral imperative. These are the tensions inherent to terrorism and they are raising important moral questions that must be explored, which is what this book will humbly try to do. I will let the readers decide whether I have been successful in this task.

Jean-François Caron
Astana, June 2022

Chapter 1
The Difficulty of Defining Terrorism

The reader is certainly accustomed to this famous quote: 'one man's terrorist is another man's freedom fighter'. In summary, this citation expresses the difficulty of defining terrorism which seems to be destined to be assessed solely from a subjective perspective. This is largely because violent struggles are first and foremost political by nature (after all, as von Clausewitz famously wrote, war is the continuation of politics by other means) and the actors involved need to get support for their respective causes which call for a necessity to identify one's fight as being just and to demonise one of the enemies. Needless to say that if the term 'freedom fighter' is associated with a noble end, 'terrorism' is for its part a highly emotional expression linked with immoral and disgusting behaviours and therefore why everybody tries to avoid being labelled as such. As a result, this way of defining terrorism ends up characterising such a myriad of situations that it has basically become a meaningless expression.

It is precisely my intention in this chapter to step aside from this subjective temptation and to distinguish terrorism from guerrilla warfare with objective criteria to make it a value-neutral expression and avoid any definition that could be dismissed as a biased political judgment. This necessary conceptual clarification will then allow the reader to have a better understanding of these two phenomena and the unique moral challenges they pose to societies and policymakers. Furthermore, assessing terrorism and guerrilla warfare differently does not mean that they do not share certain common features. In fact, it must be admitted they are very much alike when it comes to their tactics of fighting their enemies. This includes to strike at them by surprise and when they least suspect it and to create a situation where their constant harassment hinders them to foresee a rapid end to the conflict, but rather to let them reach the conclusion that holding a specific territory will be costly, both in terms of lives and from a financial viewpoint, and a political embarrassment once the public starts to criticise and oppose the mission[3]. However, these similarities cannot hide the radical eth-

---

3 This is what Bard E. O'Neill argues: 'Most insurgent leaders know they risk destruction by confronting government forces in direct conventional engagements. Instead, they opt to erode the strength of the government through the use of terrorism or guerrilla warfare, not only to increase the human and material cost to the government but also to demonstrate its failure to maintain effective control and provide protection for the people. Eventually, according to the insurgent's logic, the authorities will grow weary of the struggle and seek to prevent further losses by either capitulating or negotiating a settlement favourable to the insurgents' (2005, p. 93).

https://doi.org/10.1515/9783110757569-002

ical differences that distinguish them. These forms of political violence are not simple, interchangeable terms that can be used to describe the same reality. On the contrary, they rest on completely different sets of moral standards that are irreconcilable from one another, and assuming these two types of violence to be mere synonyms undermines their distinctiveness. To emphasise, terrorism is simply not a subcategory of guerrilla warfare, as has been rightfully highlighted by Walter Laqueur (2017, p. 5). If guerrilla is described as a form of irregular violence that abides by the moral rules of warfare (with the notable exception of guerrilla fighters not wearing distinctive uniforms), terrorism is best defined by the randomness and arbitrariness of its victims. By crossing this red line and deliberately targeting individuals indiscriminately, terrorism mostly concerns vile criminality than the legitimacy and justifiability of killing certain individuals who—for various reasons that will be discussed in the following chapter—are deemed to have lost their immunity against death.

Defining terrorism has always been a difficult intellectual endeavour and the source of numerous debates within the academic community and among policymakers. It is a debate on which complexity has simply been deepened by individuals who support the claim that terrorism also needs to be assessed differently between ancient and contemporary organisations that have chosen to exert a form of undue pressure on states through intimidation and other similar means of action to generate fear and insecurity to force a change of policy. As has been argued elsewhere (Caron, 2021), although a lot has been written about the nature of modern terrorism, many of these works are unable to specify its true nature, making it difficult to distinguish freedom fighters from terrorists. Far from being a trivial matter, if the latter notion and the means it utilises to fulfil its objectives can be morally condemned, it is not the case with the former, as this and the following chapter will show. Moreover, defining terrorism as a form of violence or a set of actions aiming to destabilise the constitutional order for the sake of political, religious, ethnic, or ideological purposes to create fear and influence a government or public body leads to a catch-all definition. This definition also encompasses the armed groups actively trying to overthrow a tyrant, groups resisting a state that is trying to mass murder its members, and organisations dispersing a highly toxic and deadly gas in the subway of a major city or high-jacking commercial airplanes before crashing them into buildings to cause as many deaths as possible. In this regard, can Michael Collins or Nelson Mandela be compared with Osama bin Laden or Abu Bakr al-Baghdadi in any manner? Alternatively, can we compare French *résistants* who fought the Nazis during WWII with Al Qaeda or ISIL fighters? I do not think this is the case. But why so?

I wish to argue that guerrilla warfare is morally distinctive from terrorism in the willingness of the former to abide by the established norms of warfare, with one of the most important being the necessity to distinguish between combatants and non-combatants[4], while terrorist organisations tend to favour the indiscriminate physical liquidation of individuals on a massive scale[5]. This distinction legitimises the fight of the former groups (under certain conditions that will be discussed at length in the following chapter), while terrorism is an immoral form of violence that cannot be justified in any manner. In this regard, it must be stated that this question of discrimination has always been a hotly debated point of divergence among individuals and groups that have historically favoured irregular ways of fighting. While some groups have openly embraced the idea of mass-murdering individuals on a massive scale, others have shown disgust and horror towards this strategy and have staunchly and vocally separated themselves from those who advocated this idea of indiscriminate killing.

Notably, from a semantic perspective, using this criterion to separate terrorists from guerrilla fighters seems practical as the term terrorism was first developed at the end of the 18th century, more specifically in France in 1793. It refers to the period when the French *révolutionnaires* implemented a regime of systematic terror that deliberately spared no one[6]. More precisely, the word was openly used by members of the *Convention nationale* who declared terror 'an order of business (*à l'ordre du jour*)' on 5 September 1793 which was followed a few days later by the adoption of the law of suspects that allowed the state to arrest anyone based on broad and imprecise criteria[7]. Saint-Just, one of Robespierre's fiercest allies, provided the basis for arrests in a speech on 10 October in which he said:

> We will not have prosperity as long as the last enemy of freedom will breathe. You must punish not only the traitors, but also those who will not be bothered; you must punish anyone who is passive in the Republic and who does not do anything for her. Ever since the

---

4 This raises a crucial question, that is who can be considered as a combatant. I will address this in the next chapter.
5 This distinction between terrorist and guerrilla groups is an implicit understanding in several studies on political violence (Carter, 2016, p. 133).
6 According to the Oxford English Dictionary, the word 'guerrilla'—a Spanish word for 'small wars'—was first introduced in English in 1809 in a dispatch from the Duke of Wellington during the Anglo-Spanish uprising against Napoleon's troops in Spain. The French referred to guerrilla warfare as '*la petite guerre*' or 'the small war'.
7 The *commune de Paris* was famous for its definition of who was to be considered a suspect. It wrote in October 1793 that: 'Those who have done nothing against freedom, also have done nothing for it'.

French people has decided to show its will, everything opposed to it ought to be considered as its enemy. We must govern with an iron fist, and we must not hesitate to oppress the tyrants (quoted in Chaliand & Blin, 2015, pp. 146 – 147).

Shortly after, the revolutionary tribunals were established that were not bound by any procedural rules and could sentence individuals unable to prove their innocence against the charges brought against them. The fact that thousands of people—a vast majority of whom were totally innocent—were sent to the guillotine shows the terroristic nature of Robespierre's regime. However, revolutionary tribunals also served another purpose, namely to spread fear throughout French society. Igor Primoratz writes:

> (...) The trials and executions were also meant to strike terror in the hearts of all those in the public at large who lacked civic virtue, and in that way coerce compliance with, and indeed active support of, revolutionary laws and policies. (...) That is what makes the "Reign of Terror" a case of state terrorism. Jacobins believed such terrorism was a necessary means of consolidating the new regime. As Robespierre put it, terror was "an emanation of virtue"; without it, virtue remained impotent. Therefore the Jacobins applied the term to their own actions and policies quite unabashedly, without any negative connotations (2013, p. 33).

This decision prefigured what was to happen in the 20th century in all totalitarian states that used similar methods. For instance, Lenin did not hesitate to order his subordinates to resort to deliberate use of indiscriminate violence against civilians[8]. Similarly, puppet tribunals under Stalin's rule tried and sentenced many under imaginary accusations. These two systems of terror were reinforced by the presence of a powerful and arbitrary secret police that could arrest individuals for any reason, resulting in the destruction of social capital. Thus, Hannah Arendt (1958, p. 464) concluded that 'terror is the essence of totalitarian domination' and Carl J. Friedrich and Zbigniew Brzezinski (1965, p. 169) wrote that 'total fear reigns' in these regimes. Therefore, it is impossible to agree with Michael

---

8 For instance, on 9th August 1918, he instructed the Soviet of Nizhni–Novgorod to act in the following way: 'It is obvious that a white-guardist uprising is being prepared in Nizhni. You must make an intense effort, appoint a troika [a team of three] of dictators, immediately proclaim mass terror, shoot and deport hundreds of prostitutes who intoxicate soldiers, former officers, etc. (...) You must act fast: mass perquisitions. Shooting for keeping of arms. Mass deportations of mensheviks and unreliables. Change the guard at the warehouses, appoint reliable ones. Yours Lenin'. Trotsky shared the same enthusiasm for this tactic. He wrote: 'terror can be very efficient against a reactionary class which does not want to leave the scene of operations. Intimidation is a powerful weapon of policy, both internationally and internally'.

Walzer's assessment that terrorism (understood as the random targeting of people) emerged as a strategy only after 1945 (2004, p. 198).

This manner of defining terrorism needs to emphasise the importance of *deliberate use of violence against innocent people* in the sense that the violence these people are victims of is not merely the result of collateral damage: a form of violence that, although sad, can nonetheless be morally justified through the just war theory. On the contrary, the deliberate violence against them as a strategy to generate political change[9] is the primary desire of terrorist groups, which defines these organisations and makes them morally wrong. This viewpoint is shared by authors such as Christopher J. Finlay, Michael Walzer, Tony Coady, Igor Primoratz, Bard E. O'Neill, and David Rosenbaum. Finlay restricts the use of the term 'terrorist' to individuals or groups who resort to deliberate violence against individuals who ought to be thought as immune from any form of violence during an armed conflict (2015, pp. 5–6). Walzer defined terrorism as follows:

> Randomness is the crucial feature of terrorist activity. If one wishes fear to spread and intensify over time, it is not desirable to kill specific people identified in some particular way with a regime, a party, or a policy. Death must come by chance to individual Frenchmen, or Germans, to Irish Protestants, or Jews, simply because they are Frenchmen or Germans, Protestants or Jews, until they feel themselves fatally exposed and demand that their governments negotiate for their safety (2004, p. 197).

This definition of terrorism has also gained some traction at the international level, especially at the United Nations that sees the core feature of this form of violence in the criterion of 'deliberate violence against civilians'. More specifically, in 2004, it has suggested to define terrorism as:

> 'Any action, in addition to actions already specified by the existing conventions on aspects of terrorism, the Geneva Conventions and Security Council resolution 1566 (2004), that is intended to cause death or serious bodily harm to civilians or non-combatants, when the purpose of such act, by its nature or context, is to intimidate a population, or to compel a government or an international organization to do or to abstain from doing any act' (United Nation, 2004, p. 52).

This definition was later supported by Kofi Annan, the former UN Secretary-General, who urged states to unite behind the notion that terrorism is a form of political violence which aims to kill civilians (Annan, 2005).

---

9 Therefore we cannot count those criminals, such as rapists or bank robbers as terrorists whose attacks against innocent civilians are not aimed at creating a political change.

Furthermore, other organisations that have also been labelled as terrorist have chosen to reject this indiscriminate logic of total war that spares none in favour of a strategy that targets only certain individuals who are deemed responsible for the establishment of the order these groups are fighting. Notably, these two morally distinctive strategies have remained at the heart of heated debates among individuals who have chosen to resort to violence against their respective states. This was especially true in the communist/anarchist ranks during the 19th century. For instance, French anarchist François-Claudius Koenigstein, aka Ravachol, who perpetrated numerous attacks between 1892 and 1894 that wounded many civilians, was severely criticised by his comrades for not respecting the discrimination between 'legitimate targets' and innocent people. That was, for instance, the case with French anarchist Émile Henry, who criticised Ravachol's actions by saying that 'the true anarchist ought to kill his enemies; but he is not doing so by blowing up houses where women, children, members of the working class and servants are living' (Chaliand & Blin, 2015, p. 172). Thus, purposely harming civilians has always been a taboo within the ranks of irregular fighters and many of them view it as a red line that should never be crossed at the risk of transforming one legitimate struggle into an immoral one.

Russian anarchists who fought Tsar's despotism also took great care not to blindly commit murder; they only targeted those who were responsible for the evil they were combating. Starting from 1866, when the first assassination attempt took place against Tsar Alexander II, Russian anarchists also targeted ministers (like Nikolay Bogolepov, Minister of National Enlightenment in 1901 or Vyacheslav von Plehve, Minister of the Interior in 1904). Moreover, when confronted with the decision to kill their target at the cost of harming innocent individuals, these terrorists decided to show restraint. This occurred in 1905, when anarchists killed Grand Duke Sergei. Two days before the fatal attack, the one chosen to pursue the mission decided not to throw the bomb when he saw that the aristocrat was accompanied by his wife and nephews, a decision that was later fully supported by his co-conspirators[10]. The same can be said about

---

10 Two months before the attempt that finally costed the life of Tsar Alexander II, he was targeted by members of the *Narodnaya Volya* organization who mistakenly blew up a train which they thought he was sitting in. As it was reported: '[one of the co-conspirators] remembered how Sofya Lvovna came to Moscow's safe house on November 19 late in the evening. Perovskaya, with a sob, threw herself on her neck, intermittently explaining, "that they had made a mistake, that they blew up the wrong train and that innocent victims were likely to have perished...". Then Sofya Lvovna fell silent and sat in silence for a long time until A.D. Mikhailov arrived. He had brought with him newspapers indicating that their action did not kill anyone. Upon receiving that news, the girls experienced an unforgettable relief and gradually began to come to

Gavrilo Princip, who showed remorse for murdering Franz Ferdinand's wife[11]. As argued by Chaliand and Blin, regardless of whether we agree with their actions, we must recognise that most of these terrorist groups followed the ethics of warfare very similar to the principle of distinction found in the *jus in bello* category that states have promised to uphold (2015, p. 228).

This attitude was opposite to that supported by like-minded anti-system individuals of that period, such as Wilhelm Weitling and Karl Heinzen, who favoured mass murder. Despite expressing his disagreement with the murder of innocents, Heinzein thought that the physical annihilation of thousands of people could serve the interests of humanity (Bessner & Stauch, 2010). He wrote: 'If you have to blow up half a continent and pour out a sea of blood in order to destroy the party of the barbarians, have no scruples of conscience. He is no true republican who would not gladly pay with his life for the satisfaction of exterminating a million barbarians' (quoted in Laqueur, 2016, p. 26). Heinzen even formulated arguments that made him the founding father of the type of terrorism that Western societies have now been confronted with over the past few decades. Moreover, his suggestions would make bin Laden and al-Baghdadi sound like mere plagiarists regarding the way indiscriminate killing ought to take place, especially with his emphasis on the necessity of using weapons of mass destruction as a key means of the revolution he was fighting for. He wrote again in February 1848: 'We have to become more energetic, more desperate [and showed great hopes in the potential of poison gas, of poisoning bullets, mines and missiles that] could destroy whole cities with 100,000 inhabitants' (quoted in Laqueur, 2016, pp. 26–27). In this regard, if Brian Orend's definition of terrorism (2013, p. 72) is not inherently problematic and is very much in line with the one I am privileging (which is "the use of violence against civilians"), it nevertheless becomes inadequate when he is associating it with 19th Century anarchists. Of course, if some of them were in favour of resorting to indiscriminate warfare, a majority of them were on the contrary opposed to such a tactic and were keen not to harm civilians.

By only attacking individuals they view as legitimate targets, guerrilla fighters therefore consider themselves different from terrorists who, because of their unwillingness to conceptualise guilt in a restrictive manner that leads to their strategy that comprises resorting to indiscriminate mass murder, cannot be re-

---

life' [translation from Russian]. https://istoriki.su/istoricheskie-temy/rossiyskaya_imperiya_v_xix_veke/620-dinamit-i-narodnaya-volya.html

11 He said: 'Yes, I am sorry that I killed the wife of Franz Ferdinand. Next to him was sitting the Governor of Bosnia and Herzegovina (Oskar Potiorek), so I shot at him. But it turned out that I killed her. For the rest, I don't regret anything'.

garded as soldiers but rather as mere criminals. From this perspective, Brazilian revolutionary Carlos Marighela wrote in his famous *Minimanual for the Urban Guerrilla* (1969):

> The urban guerrillas, however, differ radically from the criminal. The criminal benefits personally from his actions, and attacks indiscriminately without distinguishing between the exploiters and the exploited, which is why there are so many ordinary people among his victims. The urban guerrilla follows a political goal, and only attacks the government, the big businesses and the foreign imperialists.

In this regard, members of guerrilla organisations and terrorists both fight 'irregular wars', that is as non-members of regular forces of nation-states, as well as resorting to the same 'hit and hide' strategy. However, as the former entities are defined by their willingness to abide by the principle of discrimination between combatants and non-combatants tends to justify labelling them as legitimate soldiers, while the unwillingness of the latter to respect the moral rules of warfare rather contributes to transforming them as lawless offenders.

Distinguishing guerrilla from terrorism in this manner allows for a much better assessment of these two forms of political violence than any other criterion used by others, such as the role played by religion, that terrorism is strictly an affair of non-state actors, it can be defined as an irrational strategy, or that it can be solely defined by fear.

In recent times, religion has seemed to be a core element defining organisations that have been labelled as terrorist. In this regard, the Islamic Jihad, Al Qaeda, ISIL, or the Japanese sect Aum Shinrikyo that became famous for its deadly Tokyo subway sarin attack of 1995 that killed 14 people and injured more than a thousand innocent civilians. However, understanding terrorism through this prism is problematic as it presupposes two inaccurate premises: 1) that terrorism is a contemporary phenomenon and 2) that it is impossible to understand terrorism without associating it with religion. Both these premises are problematic if we choose to define terrorism through the lens of indiscriminate killing. First, religion has always been a driving force behind the mobilisation of groups that have resorted to irregular means of warfare. Furthermore, not only did religious beliefs on the part of these groups not always lead them to favour a strategy of indiscriminate killing, but the aforementioned examples of Ravachol, Wilhelm Weitling, and Karl Heinzen also clearly show that the terrorist phenomenon is not necessarily associated with religion.

In this vein, the best examples are those of the Sicarii, Assassins, and Thugs. The Sicarii are usually remembered as one of the first terrorist movements that were active in Palestine from 66 to 73 A.D. When surrounded by the Romans in the fortress of Masada, they choose to commit suicide rather than surrender to their enemies. Their opposition to the Roman authorities stemmed from their Messianic belief that only God should be their ruler and the only authority they ought to submit to rather than obey an empire based on pagan beliefs and the idolatry of its rulers. More specifically, 'This empire was the complete antithesis of the spiritual conception and way of life of the Jews, and the tension found its resolution in the strengthening of a messianic-eschatological faith at the centre of which stood the hope of the revival of the glory of Israel and the downfall of 'the kingdom of arrogance' (Stern). Despite bearing the label of a terrorist organisation, the Sicarii do not fit the definition presented previously as their numerous acts of violence were not indiscriminate. Contrarily, they purposely targeted only the Roman 'invaders' and their Jewish collaborators, who were identified as traitors, which took the form of an urban guerrilla. According to the Romano–Jewish historian Titus Flavius Josephus, the Sicarii's main tactic was the public assassination of political and religious public figures to create a general feeling of insecurity in Judea using a small dagger (called a *sicae*) concealed under their clothes[12].

Furthermore, the Assassins, the members of a Shia Islam sect who operated in the Middle East and its neighbouring regions during the 11th and 13th centuries, functioned in a similar manner. Described as a 'deviant religious group' from mainstream Islam (Rapoport, 1984, pp. 659–660), this group was organised around a mysticism and esoterism that were deemed unorthodox by other Muslims. Similarly to the Sicarii, the Assassins (namely those known as *fida'i* within the sect) also publicly assassinated figures who were leading the charge against their divine mission. Additionally, they favoured the discriminate killing of these specific individuals and never advocated for the mass murder of civilians. Their most famous murder is that of Nizam al-Mulk, the vizier of the Seljuk Empire in

---

12 As Josephus wrote: 'But while the country was thus cleared of these pests, a new species of banditti was springing up in Jerusalem, the so-called sicarii, who committed murders in broad daylight in the heart of the city. The festivals were their special seasons, when they would mingle with the crowd, carrying short daggers concealed under their clothing, with which they stabbed their enemies. Then, when they fell, the murderers joined in the cries of indignation and, through this plausible behaviour, were never discovered. The first to be assassinated by them was Jonathan the high-priest; after his death there were numerous daily murders. The panic created was more alarming than the calamity itself: every one, as on the battlefield, hourly expecting death. Men kept watch at a distance on their enemies and would not trust even their friends when they approached. Yet, even while their suspicions were aroused and they were on their guard, they fell; so swift were the conspirators and so crafty in eluding detection' (Jewish War, Book. 2, par. 252–258).

1092, which remains one of the first major terrorist attacks[13]. Subsequent murders included that of Conrad of Montferrat, King of Jerusalem, in 1192, as well as two unsuccessful attempts against Saladin.

Moreover, other groups whose fights originated from religious beliefs made different strategic choices and adopted means of warfare that led to the indiscriminate killing of thousands of individuals. Their 'Holy Terror' purpose comprised forcing their victims to experience terror and express it publicly before being killed for the pleasure of Kali, the Hindu goddess of terror and destruction[14], to retain balance in the universe (Sedgwick, 2004, p. 798). During the long time period during which they terrified the territories on which they operated, it is estimated that the Thugs killed approximately 500,000 to one million individuals during the last three centuries of their history[15]: a conservative esti-

---

13 As reported by Ata-Malek Juvayni in his *History of the Word Conqueror:* 'Now at the time when Hasan first rose in rebellion Nizam-al-Mulk Hasan b. 'Ali b. Ishaq of Tus (may God have mercy on him!) was Malik-Shah's vizier. With his penetrating glance he beheld on the features of the actions wrought by Hasan-i-Sabbah and his followers the signs of troubles in Islam and perceived therein the indications of disturbances; and he strove his hardest to excise the pus of the Sabbahian rebellion and exerted every effort in equipping and dispatching troops to suppress and subdue them. Hasan-i-Sabbah spread the snare of artifices in order at the first opportunity to catch some splendid game, such as Nizam-al-Mulk, in the net of destruction and increase thereby his own reputation. With the juggling of deceit and the trickery of falsehood, with absurd preparations and spurious deceptions, he laid the basis of the fida'is. A person called Bu-Tahir, Arrani by name and by origin, was afflicted "with the loss both of this world and of the next", and in his misguided striving after bliss in the world to come on the night of Friday the 12th of Ramazan, [6th of October, 1092] he went up to Nizam-al-Mulk's litter at a stage called Sahna in the region of Nihavand. Nizam-al-Mulk, having broken the fast, was being borne in the litter from the Sultan's audience-place to the tent of his harem. Bu-Tahir who was disguised as a Sufi, stabbed him with a dagger and by that blow Nizam-al-Mulk was martyred. He was the first person to be killed by the fida'is. (...) And from then onwards he used to cause the emirs, commanders and notables to be assassinated by his fida'is one after the other. On this account the local rulers (afbab-i-atraf), near and far, were exposed to danger and would fall into the whirl pool of destruction' (1958, pp. 676–678).

14 David C. Rapoport writes: 'For obscure religious reasons Thugs attacked only travellers, and although they confiscated the property of their victims, material gain was not their principal concern (...). The legend of their origin also shows murder to be the Thugs' main business, murder in which the death agony was deliberately prolonged to give Kali ample time to enjoy the terror expressed by the victims' (1984, p. 662).

15 Rapoport writes: 'No one knows exactly when the Thugs (often called Phansigars or stranglers) first appeared. Few now believe that the ancient Sagartians, whom Herodotus describes as stranglers serving in the Persian army, are the people whom the British encountered in India some 2500 years later. But there is evidence that Thugs existed in the seventh century, and almost all scholars agree that they were vigorous in the thirteenth, which means that the group persisted for at least six hundred years' (p. 661).

mate that is beyond the combined number of people killed by contemporary terrorist organisations.

These case studies clearly show that religion does not always lead to a form of holy terror or the indiscriminate killing of people. On the contrary, the Sicarii and Assassins exhibit that a group whose ideology is intimately connected with religious beliefs can end up privileging means of warfare that can be labelled in the guerrilla logic. Whereas the previously mentioned cases of Ravachol, Weitling, and Heinzen illustrate, how terrorism sometimes has nothing to do with religion. Consequently, although tempting considering contemporary terrorist groups that are clearly animated by the logic of the Holy Terror, religion cannot simply be considered a defining feature of terrorism.

Furthermore, terrorism has been defined through the distinction between state and non-state actors with the belief that this form of political violence was the sole feature of the latter entities. As previously argued, such an understanding of terrorism is clearly a way for states to give themselves the moral high ground by demonising their enemies by labelling them as terrorists as if only their own political violence was legitimate. This assessment is inaccurate, especially considering the origins of the word 'terrorism' that was linked with state actors during the French Revolution.

In fact, it is a mistake to think of terrorism and its indiscriminate use of violence only as the purview of non-state actors. Additionally, it should be stressed that what Gérard Chaliand and Arnaud Blin (2015, p. 21) have labelled 'top-down terrorism (*terrorisme d'en haut*)' has actually led to exponentially more deaths than 'grassroots terrorism (*terrorisme d'en bas*)'. Regarding state-sponsored terrorism (as was the case with Libya under Gaddafi or Iran, which have directly or indirectly engaged in violence against citizens or other states), we should not neglect the fact that totalitarian states have also made terrorism a core feature of their domestic politics. It is precisely this former form of terrorism that justified in Heinzen's mind the resort to mass murder of people by non-state actors. He is indeed recalling in his writings the hypocrisy of states that condemn and express moral outrage when terrorist groups commit indiscriminate killings but do not hesitate to do the same and in much greater proportions. In his mind, what is good for the goose is good for the gander as well and the only thing that made this reality acceptable is simply the capacity of states to morally justify murders because they have the power to legalise it, while condemning to the gallows those who were too weak to do the same by labelling them as terrible and immoral criminals. From this perspective, he reminds his readers of the following historical examples:

Following the final victory of Crassus over the slaves under Spartacus, 6,000 of the same were nailed to a double row of crosses that graced the streets from Rome to Capua. Trajan, following his victory over the Dacians, allowed 10,000 slaves to appear as gladiators in the circus of Rome and fight with 11,000 wild animals; that is, he allowed an army of men and an army of animals to kill each other simply for pleasure. Potemkin allowed 30,000 Tartars (men, women, and children) to be captured and massacred because they refused to "render homage" to Queen Catherine. In the Netherlands, Alba allowed 18,000 people to be "executed." Charles the "Great" exterminated almost the entire people of Saxony in order to convert it. The "Christians" murdered hundreds of thousands of Albigenses; in the city of Beziores alone 6,000 of the same were put down. By means of the Inquisition the priests murdered hundreds of thousands in cold blood. At the St. Bartholomew's Day Massacre, because of which the high murderer in Rome, the Pope, decreed a jubilee year, 30,000 Protestants were murdered. In the Peasant Wars, 150,000 peasants were murdered. And so forth, and so forth. If we go through the murder ledger of history, we find the most acts of murder on the account of Christianity, the "religion of love." In the name of Christianity perhaps more people have been ferried to "that other world" than there currently are believing Christians upon this world, such that Christ manifested an admirable foresight when he said: "My kingdom is not of this world." He could have with good reason said: My kingdom is the graveyard (quoted in Bessner & Stauch, 2010).

Moreover, state terrorism has also been the appanage of democratic states that have not hesitated to proceed with indiscriminate means of violence. For instance, the decision by Winston Churchill and Arthur 'Bomber' Harris, the commander-in-chief of the Bomber Command during WWII, to proceed to 'area bombings' of German cities—a euphemism for the large-scale indiscriminate bombings of cities with the sole aim of terrorising the population and crushing morale—was clearly a case of state terror[16].

---

16 In this regard, we can quote Churchill's famous 8th July 1940 letter to Lord Beaverbrook, the Minister of Aircraft Production, in which he wrote: 'In the fierce light of the present emergency the fighter is the need, and the output of fighters must be the prime consideration till we have broken the enemy's attack. But when I look round to see how we can win the war, I see that there is only one sure path. We have no Continental army which can defeat the German military power. The blockade is broken and Hitler has Asia and probably Africa to draw from. Should he be repulsed here or not try invasion, he will recoil eastward, and we have nothing to stop him. But there is one thing that will bring him back and bring him down, and that is an absolutely devastating, exterminating attack by very heavy bombers from this country upon the Nazi homeland. We must be able to overwhelm them by this means, without which I do not see a way through. We cannot accept any lower aim than air mastery. When can it be obtained?'. Churchill was fully aware of the immoral nature of these bombings, which was emphasised in his 28th March 1945 letter to General Ismay following the bombing of Dresden in the closing weeks of the war. He wrote: 'It seems to me that the moment has come when the question of bombing of German cities simply for the sake of increasing the terror, though under other pretexts, should be reviewed. Otherwise we shall come into control of an utterly ruined land. We shall not, for instance, be able to get housing materials out of Germany for our own needs because some tem-

Therefore, defining terrorism as a tool solely used by non-state actors is misleading. History has shown that the indiscriminate use of violence has also been a feature of state actors, leading to a significantly greater number of deaths than when used by non-state actors. Additionally, even though the Holocaust or the massacre of the civilians of Srebrenica in the summer of 1995 have generally been labelled as state or state-sponsored genocides, they ought to be considered as acts of terrorism. It is also incorrect to restrict the logic of terrorism to non-democratic states as democracies have also resorted to this type of violence in the past, as it was clearly a strategy openly advocated by Great Britain during WWII.

Furthermore, linking terrorism to state actors also allows us to counter other misconceptions that people may have about terrorism, namely, that it is a form of pressure to enact a desired change. There are several examples of state terrorism that show how this form of political violence is not always linked to a form of 'progressivism', but rather with a conservative desire to prevent a change from occurring. In this regard, we can think of the South African government's violent actions against its black citizens in its efforts to avert the end of its apartheid regime.

It is also incorrect to suppose that terrorism is characterised by its members' irrationality and lack of strategic thinking. Although I am not denying that it may be the case, especially with those abiding by a logic of 'Holy Terror', nonetheless the resort to terroristic tactics may also be the result of a cold and rational calculation. As previously stated, the tactics of irregular warfare used both by guerrilla groups and terrorists stem from the same assessment of reality: they are facing an overwhelmingly stronger enemy who they cannot defeat in a conventional battle by concentrating all their forces at a specific time and place to win a decisive battle. Similarly to the tactics behind non-violent resistance (Holmes, 1989, pp. 260 – 294), resorting to elusive methods of fighting is the only solution they can consider to negate their enemy's superiority and by forcing them to change their course of action as the resistance from the guerrilla/terrorist group makes it no longer profitable by draining its administrative and military manpower. This method, which has been summarised in the *Handbook for Volunteers of the Irish*

---

porary provision would have to be made for the Germans themselves. The destruction of Dresden remains a serious query against the conduct of Allied bombing. I am of the opinion that military objectives must henceforth be more strictly studied in our own interest rather than that of the enemy. The Foreign Secretary has spoken to me on this subject, and I feel the need for more precise concentration upon military objectives, such as oil and communications behind the immediate battle-zone, rather than on mere acts of terror and wanton destruction, however impressive'.

Republican Army Notes on Guerrilla Warfare (also known as the 'Green Book' (1956)), also applies to terrorist organisations. It states:

> A small nation fighting for freedom can only hope to defeat an oppressor or occupying power by means of guerrilla warfare. The enemy's superiority in manpower, resources, materials, and everything else that goes into the waging of successful war can only be overcome by the correct application of guerrilla methods (Chapter 2). The guerrilla will not fight the enemy in a long battle where reserves would overwhelm him: he strikes only when he can win. And he avoids superior forces. When the enemy advances, he withdraws. When the enemy rests, he hits him. He attacks when the enemy is exhausted. And when the enemy counterattacks, the guerrilla flees (Chapter 4). The regular soldier is no match for the trained guerrilla in attack. Because the guerrilla holds the initiative, strikes when he is ready, uses shock action and surprise to attain his ends, then breaks contact and withdraws (Chapter 8).

Josip Broz alias Tito, who led the partisan uprising against the Germans in occupied Yugoslavia during WWII, shared similar views. He confessed to Brigadier sir Fitzroy McLean, who had unprecedented access to him as Churchill's personal representative, that if the goal was to strike as hard as possible against the Germans, it was also important for Tito's men to deny the enemy any target to strike back. Due to their low number of fighters—at least in the initial stages of the resistance—the partisans had to rely on surprise and shock attacks rather than pitched battles that would have resulted in them being wiped out by the superior German military (Polk, 2008, p. 85). A similar tactic was advocated by Carlos Marighela, whose theories on urban guerrilla warfare resembled those of the IRA. Surprise attacks with lightning results, unconventional methods, and draining of the enemy's will to pursue combat were the chief words found in his manual. Consequently, guerrilla and terrorist groups are usually organised in a similar fashion, that is, through decentralised cells independent from one another and composed of very few individuals (15 to 25 men). These groups usually decide on their own targets and how to carry out strategic shock attacks without receiving orders from a central command or any outside help. This was the case with the IRA's flying columns and with terrorists who planned and executed the 2004 and 2005 attacks in Madrid and London. Their goal is to shock the enemy by perpetrating what first appears to be an impossible task. Owing to the risk of information leaks, only in exceptional circumstances will these groups be called on by this central authority to undertake certain operations, as was the case with the 9/11 attacks by Al Qaeda operatives, as well as on 27 August 1979 when the IRA killed in a coordinated attack at two separate locations both Lord Mountbatten and 18 British soldiers in an ambush now known as the Warrenpoint ambush.

Guerrilla groups tend to think of themselves as the spearhead of the cause they are fighting for and as educators by exposing the lies of their enemy. This means that gaining and maintaining people's support is essential to their success, a task that is made challenging by the fact that ultimately the population will most likely bear the weight of the enemy's retaliation measures. To succeed, guerrilla groups will therefore need to have strong ties with the civilian population to win their trust by converting the people to their cause and by supporting and helping them when they are the victims of the enemy's actions. However, when insurgents pose actions that prove detrimental to civilians, the latter no longer harbour them and provide them with food or any other form of assistance. For these groups, victory is not considered possible without support[17]. As Mao famously stated, to succeed, a guerrilla group is like a fish that needs water to survive; in this case, water refers to popular support. When water runs dry because of ill-fated indiscriminate attacks that may cost the lives of innocent civilians, the terrorist fish will be doomed to starve and die.

Alongside the moral reasons that justify in their mind the necessity of discriminating between legitimate targets and non-combatants/civilians[18], the requirement to maintain civilian support further explains the selectiveness of their targets and attacks. Moreover, through their tactics of surprise shock attacks, guerrilla groups are also able to gain civilian support because their actions provoke an imprecise and indiscriminate response from the state forces that further reinforces the propaganda concerning the immorality of the state they are opposing. Bloody Sunday of 1920 that led to the death of 30 people—some killed in a stadium during a Gaelic football match—is a good example because it was a response to the assassination of 15 British undercover agents by Michael Collins's men the day before. Consequently, this act of senseless and indiscriminate retaliation increased support for the IRA and radicalised public opinion (Hopkinson, 2004, p. 91; English, 2003, p. 17). As empirical analysis has shown, these groups that resort to either guerrilla or terrorist violence are especially good at selecting such means of action that will simultaneously limit the states' capacity to retaliate precisely and effectively against their members and increase the likelihood that the state's retaliation will harm civilians (Carter, 2016). In this case, by resorting to terroristic tactics, entities targeted by these insurgents are digging

---

17 This necessity had been identified in the earliest known work on guerrilla warfare by Sextus Julius Frontinius (who died in 103 AD) that the success of guerrilla groups depended on the support of the local population (see Segdwick, 2004, p. 801).

18 A necessity that was, for instance, very important for Ernesto 'Che' Guevara who saw terrorism and indiscriminate killing of people as an ineffective and immoral strategy (2007, p. 17).

their own graves by increasing the support for these groups and the number of people willing to fight for them, as discussed by William Polk:

> When the dominant government seeks to suppress [these insurgents], two things frequently happen. Almost inevitably the government disrupts the lives of innocent bystanders and hurts or kills still more. In 1808 in Spain Napoleon's soldiers routinely hanged all rebels they caught and those suspected of favoring them. The relatives and friends of the hanged quickly came to hate the French. Against the Philippine rebels, first the Spaniards and then the American undertook search and destroy operations that killed thousands of people in the 1890s, tortured or humiliated many more, and burned scores of villages. Doing so triggered Philippine resistance. In Yugoslavia during the Second World War, the Germans employed a draconian system of reprisals, executing not only all the partisans they captured but hundreds of civilian hostages in retaliation for the death of each German soldier. The relatives, neighbours, and friends of those killed by foreign troops sought revenge, and the place to get it was in the ranks of the insurgents. So from a handful, their numbers grew (Polk, 2008, pp. xix – xx).

Groups that are operating on the territory they wish to free from the oppression they oppose must therefore be sensitive to maintaining the support of the people by carefully avoiding harming civilians during their shock attack. This may explain why the ETA largely used guerrilla tactics rather than terrorist acts in Northern Ireland and Spain, or in the 1960s in Quebec with the *Front de libération du Québec*. Furthermore, groups operating on foreign soil and bringing combat to the heart of their enemy's territory may not have this sensitivity, as those who might be killed are not considered 'their people' and, accordingly, they are unconcerned if resorting to terrorism against them results in their loss of support, which they do not require in the first place. Till such actions are welcomed by their own people, resorting to indiscriminate violence may appear in their eyes to be the best strategy. For instance, the 1995 bombings in France, carried out by the Armed Islamic Group of Algeria, who planted handmade explosive devices in the Parisian metropolitan train system, that killed eight and injured 157; radical Palestinian organisations that undertook suicide attacks on buses and restaurants in Israeli territory following the second intifada; and the 9/11 attacks by Al Qaeda. However, this may not always be an efficient way to understand why groups opt for either guerrilla or terrorist tactics.

We may be tempted to argue that religion plays a pivotal role in the choice between guerrilla tactics and indiscriminate targeting of individuals. Indeed, the necessity to act strategically is different for groups animated by a transcendental apocalyptic understanding of the world. Groups organised around this latter belief think of their cause as being self-sufficient and of themselves as the instruments at the service of the sacred cause they are pursuing. As everything else is thought to be subordinate to their cause (which includes the judgment of others), their violence has no limitations. In this regard, we can consider the Thugs whose only aim was to please their goddess Kali or the deadly Tokyo subway sarin gas attack in 1995 by members of the Aum Shinrikyo sect who attacked their own people[19]. In this case, its leader had predicted Armageddon by 1997, following the start of a war between the West and the 'Buddhist World' led by Asia during which the forces of evil would destroy themselves and that only the chosen ones would survive (Metraux, 1995, p. 115 – 1153). Its leader, Shoko Asahara, perceived the attack as a way to usher in Armageddon and offer salvation to those who would die from it. Indeed, 'By initiating Armageddon Asahara believed that since Aum's enlightened members were performing the killings, the victims would be purified at their moment of death and would therefore receive the best possible chance of attaining rebirth in one of the higher realms' (Nicholls, 2007, p. 35). This is also true for Hezbollah, which sees the death of its enemies as a godly act. When such a mentality predominates, terrorism is more likely to prevail over guerrilla tactics, irrespective of whether the group is operating at home or on foreign soil.

However, linking terrorism to irrational 'Holy Terror' is problematic. In addition to the fact that the indiscriminate targeting of individuals played a central role in the actions of Ravachol and other 19th century anarchists, this option has also been privileged by groups of national liberation that have seen terrorism as a sound strategy. While some groups may realise that terrorism is strategically counter-productive, as it tends to alienate the population from the cause they are fighting for, others may conclude that a provocation strategy aimed at targeting their enemy indiscriminately will ultimately be favourable to their cause. This is, for instance, the strategy used by the Armenians at the end of the 19th century and, more recently, when they chose to attack Ottoman/Turkish civilians[20]. However, their strategy did not lead to the expected outcome. As Laqueur wrote:

---

19 Bruce Hoffman wrote about terrorist groups abiding by a 'Holy Terror' that: 'For the religious terrorist, violence first and foremost is a sacramental act or divine duty executed in direct response to some theological demand or imperative. Terrorism assumes a transcendental dimension, and its perpetrators are therefore unconstrained by the political, moral, or practical constraints that seem to affect other terrorists' (1993, p. 2). Audrey Cronin wrote that terrorist actions from these groups are solely aimed at 'pleas[ing] the perceived commands of a deity' (2002/03, p. 41).

20 For instance, the Armenian Secret Army for the Liberation of Armenia staged indiscriminate attacks in numerous locations worldwide, such as in Turkey (the 1982 Esenboga airport attack) or France (the 1983 Orly airport attack). Notably, this indiscriminate strategy of violence led to a schism within the movement between those in favour of it and those who opposed it and only supported attacks against representatives of the Turkish government.

> The proponents of immediate action prevailed, and since they could not possibly hope to overthrow the government, their strategy had to be based on provocation. They assumed, in all probability, that their attacks on the Turks would provoke savage retaliation, and that as a result the Armenian population would be radicalized; more decisive yet, the Western powers, appalled by the massacres, would intervene on their behalf as they did for the Bulgarians two decades earlier. Lastly, they seem to have hoped that their example would lead to risings among other nationalities in the Ottoman empire, as well as perhaps inspiring disaffected Turks. Their most spectacular action was the seizure of the Ottoman Bank in Constantinople in August 1896. But the results were disastrous: a three-day massacre followed in which thousands of Armenians were killed [and] Europe showed "murderous indifference" (Laqueur, 2017, p. 44).

Some terroristic actions perpetrated by Al-Qaeda-affiliated individuals were also undertaken with a strategic purpose. For instance, the 2004 attack in Madrid's train stations was primarily aimed at shocking the Spanish population to lead them to oppose their country's intervention in Iraq following the US-led invasion the year before. In these cases, the deliberate indiscriminate targeting of people is not an end in itself, but rather a simple yet horrible means to achieve a specific political goal. In the same vein, the desire to provoke a strong retaliation from the United States to generate additional support for its cause was also a part of Al Qaeda's plan in September 2001. Indeed, as argued by Mark Sedgwick:

> The potential supporters of Al Qaeda's desired insurrection (against regimes such as the Saudi one and against the United States) are, of course, the world's Muslims, or at least the world's Arabs. To the world's Arabs, 9/11 certainly demonstrated the vulnerability of the United States in the most dramatic fashion. By its responses in Afghanistan and—especially—in Iraq, the United States then alienated Al Qaeda's target audience from the United States (...). There were many justifications for those responses, but their impact on the Arab world has been reminiscent of the impact of British policy on Ireland in the aftermath of the Easter Rising. To the average Arab, the toppling of the Taliban in Afghanistan appeared as an act of revenge on the people of Afghanistan, and the invasion of Iraq appeared as an unprovoked attack on a long-suffering people whose only crime was to be Arab and Muslim (Sedgwick, 2004, p. 803).

Such a strategy is, however, a double-edged sword because it may not lead the victims of such a terrorist attack to resort to indiscriminate killings. In this case, only the terrorist group will suffer international reprobation, which will lead to long-lasting and permanent reputational harm to its cause. This may explain, in part, why guerrilla groups that are commonly referred to as 'national liberation groups', such as the IRA or the ETA in Spain, have historically shown great care in designing and planning their attacks. In such instances, these groups fight another entity to either establish their own country or impose their ideology. Additionally, they are aware that their political goal's success will eventually require the support and recognition of international actors, thus they cannot afford the risk of being labelled as terrorists as this would dramatically hinder their capacity to achieve their objectives. However, the fact that terrorism has been the privileged tactic of religious groups whose actions were dictated by an apocalyptic worldview or by a willingness to abide by their religious doctrines without considering the harm it may do to their cause should not blind us to the fact that resorting to this tactic can also result from a rational strategic calculation. Moreover, it is inaccurate to argue that terrorism solely belongs to the irrational domain.

Other authors, such as Peter R. Neumann (2009) or T.P. Thornton (1964), have chosen to define terrorism through the lens of 'fear', namely as 'the deliberate creation of fear, usually through the use (or threat to use) of symbolic acts of violence, to influence the political behaviours of a target group' (Neumann, 2009, p. 8). However, this definition has several flaws. Considering the previous arguments, it tends to create a catch-all understanding of all forms of violence that leaves us unable to distinguish between genuine forms of terrorism from those associated with guerrilla warfare, thereby bringing us back to the subjective assessment of who is a freedom fighter and who is a terrorist. It is a mistake to confuse bin Laden and Jean Moulin in the same category, and as I will explain in more detail in the next chapter, it is necessary to make such a distinction.

Furthermore, associating 'fear' with 'terrorism' is also problematic as it gives to the former notion an entirely negative moral connotation that ought to be condemned. In contrast, fear, that is the fear of being punished, serves an important societal purpose. Indeed, modern reflection has been profoundly anchored from Machiavelli to Michel Foucault in the need for people to fear being punished by the state as the only way to maintain peace, order, and stability within political associations (Caron, 2019a). Indeed, if men are naturally thought to always prioritise what is good for themselves, even if it comes at the expense of others' rights or interests (Caron, 2019b, p. 13), the possibility of being able to organise social life depends upon the capacity to hinder their selfishness and find ways to force them to consider their individual actions within their broader societal context and the others' interests. According to this realistic assessment of human nature, this can be achieved in several ways. For instance, in the context of a democratic republic, Machiavelli thought that the power of the law, development of a complex set of countermeasures that might prevent one group from imposing its views on other groups with diverging interests, a sense of patriotism, or an astute use of religion were all means of achieving the well-needed pacification of human relations[21]. In this regard, if we follow Neumann's definition, laws and other state decrees would have to be considered under the umbrella of terrorism, which of course does not make any sense. This would lead to a definition that would include judges who impose harsh sanctions on individuals hoping to deter others from following the same criminal path or instructors like myself who threaten students that their assessments would not be graded if they submit after the deadline, or to expel them from the classrooms if they use their smartphones during lectures (Wellmann, 1979). I have some concerns about correlating the need for civility, professionalism, and the need to prevent felonies with terrorism. Pursuing that view would result in transforming all societies and all individuals[22] into terrorist entities, thereby preventing us from distinguishing legitimate forms of coercion and fear from others. Furthermore, if fear can be a misused tool by entities to scare their citizens and deny them unfairly their most basic freedom, it is also a legitimate way of creating peace, order, and stability in any given society.

Additionally, in the sphere of international relations, fear is also a banal form of coercion between states that undertakes numerous actions that are not considered to be morally problematic or acts of war. This is especially the case with what James Pattison has labelled as 'alternatives to war' (2018), which is a non-violent form of pressure imposed on states to force them to change their policy. Similarly to many UN resolutions, these 'measures short of war' usually serve as warnings against entities not abiding by international norms and incorporating a large spectrum of non-violent or 'soft war' actions (Gross, 2015; Gross & Meisels, 2017). For example, diplomatic and economic sanctions, or imposing embargoes on the exportation of arms and weapons to these countries. Ultimately, these measures are often a prelude to war when they have proved ineffective in resolving the issue at hand.

It is clear that such coercive measures can be abused by rogue states to exert undue pressure on their neighbours so that they may have to give away territories to avoid facing an invasion. However, sometimes these forms of pressure against rogue or aggressive states are set forward by the international community. In this case, they are legitimate warnings that harsher measures— which can

---

21 In the context where political power ought to be temporarily concentrated in the hands of one ruler when circumstances require it—which is how his *Prince* ought to be read and understood (Caron, 2019cd)—the individual in charge must be feared by the citizens who must be aware that any actions on their part that might jeopardize public order will be severely punished.

22 In all honesty, rare are the persons who can claim to have never intimidated another person in their lives.

go up to war itself—are on the agenda if they do not alter their course of action and if they do not comply with the international community. In such cases, like a state posing a threat to the lives of its citizens, this form of fear can be deemed permissible and even welcomed. However, Neumann's definition erases the normative difference between a dictator threatening its neighbour of war and the international community menacing Gaddafi's Libya of an armed attack if he does not refrain from killing innocent protesters by assuming that fear is a moral calamity.

Furthermore, we may question the desire to eliminate fear in politics. It is perfectly understandable for people and states to want to live in a peaceful world untampered with the fear of seeing one's security being challenged. However, simultaneously, we cannot ignore the fact that it is not only an unachievable political dream, as it is in the nature of other states to always seek to maximise their power and influence over other entities; but also not desirable for societies. As argued centuries ago by Augustine, a small dose of fear can be highly beneficial to societies as it helps develop well-needed social virtues, namely vigilance and a willingness to protect and defend institutions that allow people to be free and enjoy basic human rights[23]. In contrast, when individuals are no longer fearful, there is a risk that they might lower their guard and be unable to foresee a real threat from arising. For Augustine, it is precisely this lack of vigilance caused by their lack of fear (which led to *apatheia*) on the part of Roman citizens that favoured the conflicts between Marius and Sulla or Pompey and Caesar (*The City of God*, I.30). In our liberal democratic era, following the well-known arguments of Benjamin Constant and Alexis de Tocqueville, the fear of statesmen abusing their power and depriving us of our freedom, forces us to remain vigilant to all their comings and goings. Inevitably, there is an undeniable value in fear and it cannot, accordingly, be solely associated with the immorality of terrorist violence.

My arguments thus far bring us back to an ongoing debate within the academic community regarding the differences between old and new terrorism, with the latter being transnational by nature, more violent and animated by a form of 'Holy Terror'. However, if we accept the distinction I have suggested be-

---

23 As a Christian thinker, Augustine primarily saw in fear a capacity to elevate men so they could reach the City of God. As J. Warren Smith wrote in this regard: 'the struggle against fear is part of God's training humanity in the way of true justice. Rather than escaping fear by eliminating its temporal causes, Augustine argues that we must live with our fear so as to place our hope upon the kingdom to come. There is a sense that living with fear is living with the reality of death and the threat of our judgment by God. Living with such knowledge cultivates humility' (2007, pp. 149–150).

tween guerrilla warfare and terrorism, we need to agree that the latter form of political violence has not essentially evolved over time, which makes a discussion about old and new forms of terrorism useless in my opinion.

First, there are reasons to question the idea according to which a shift has appeared over the last 25 years or so that has seen terrorist organisations becoming more religiously motivated and is unconstrained by any limits on the use of violence, even weapons of mass destruction (Simon & Benjamin, 2000). More specifically, Peter R. Neumann stated that while old terrorist organisations' aims were mainly nationalist and/or Marxist, their contemporary counterparts are religiously inspired and that while they previously respected the rules of warfare by striking only against legitimate targets, today's groups attack indiscriminately (Neumann, 2009, p. 29). Considering the previously mentioned arguments about the role that religion has historically played in the *modus operandi* of terrorist organisations, it seems obvious that this first feature that ought to characterise contemporary terrorism is not a novelty at all. Furthermore, there are plenty of examples from the past that show how terrorism has indiscriminately targeted individuals irrespective of who they were. Arguing otherwise is a sign of the ability to distinguish guerrilla groups from terrorist organisations. Accordingly, presenting a feature that has always defined a phenomenon as a novelty is problematic and would be like claiming that cheese is the new ingredient that is redefining our knowledge of the... cheesecake recipe that was invented during the antiquity.

I will, however, agree that the use (or the threat of using) of weapons of mass destruction is a new type of danger that societies that have been historically targeted by terrorist organisations did not have to face. If members of these organisations usually relied on knives, guns, and bombs to fulfil their immoral strategy, their contemporary counterparts have not hesitated from using commercial airliners or chemical agents (as was the case with the Aum Shinrikyo sect) against their enemies. However, besides the unrestricted use of all methods of warfare (including weapons of mass destruction) that was advocated by terrorist thinkers in the 19th century, the comparison between the period when 'old terrorist organizations' operated and the current one, must also consider the availability of the types of weapons groups had at their disposal then compared to now. In other words, it would be harebrained to argue that the Thugs were less violent than members of the Aum Shinrikyo because the former did not use chemical agents to kill their enemies or transform commercial airliners into fuel-filled missiles against skyscrapers. They may have used the same weapon had they gotten the chance. Therefore, to fairly compare groups that operated at different time periods, the question is whether these groups used the most extreme means of killing at their disposal at the time they operated. This is the only way to evaluate the degree of brutality between groups that are sometimes separated by centuries. However, it is possible to have reservations in this regard. Regarding top-down terrorism, it is clear that states have very often used the most indiscriminate and terrible ways of killing at their disposal. For instance French *révolutionnaires* Joseph Fouché and Jean-Marie Collot d'Herbois, who exerted total terror in Lyon during their mission in 1793 by killing individuals strapped together with grapeshot fired from cannons or Jean-Baptiste Carrier, his colleague at the *Convention nationale,* who drowned mixed individuals (sometimes priests and nuns) attached together by throwing them in the Loire River (which were later called 'the Republican marriages'). Churchill's area bombings of German cities were also realised with some of the most awful and cruel weapons of the time, such as highly explosive and incendiary bombs that transformed entire cities into infernos. For instance, allied pilots who participated in Operation Gomorrha, which destroyed Hamburg and killed at least 45,000 civilians in the summer of 1943, reported to have been able to smell the odour of burned human flesh from their plane flying at 20,000 feet. When it comes to grassroots terrorism, it is also difficult to see a radical shift considering that, despite not having weapons of mass destruction at their disposal, the Thugs managed to kill between 500,000 and one million individuals in the course of their terrorist history with rudimentary weapons.

If we agree that terrorism stands for the indiscriminate targeting of people who have done nothing to justify their loss of immunity against a violent death, we must admit that the terrorist actions we witnessed in the second half of the 20th century do not constitute a paradigmatic shift when it comes to the political violence of non-state actors. Throughout history, tension has always existed between this form of violence and that of the guerrilla groups. Additionally, terrorism is by no means an exclusively contemporary phenomenon, as many groups, such as the Thugs, have used indiscriminate harm against people in a way that was similar to the actions of Al Qaeda, the Islamic State, or the Aum Shinrikyo sect.

Others have argued that if a shift between old and new forms of terrorism can be identified, it is probably the fact that an increasing number of these groups are now operating from a territory they are either controlling themselves or thanks to the assistance of state entities, as was the case with ISIL and Al Qaeda prior to the 9/11 attacks. This would mark for Laqueur the 'beginning of a new form of terrorism' (2018, p. 94). Needless to say, such a reality is highly problematic, as it now allows these groups to use all the benefits associated with territoriality instead of having to live in clandestinity that condemned them to small-scale attacks. Will this trend be short-lived, or is it indeed the beginning of a new reality that state will have to cope with in the future? It may be too early to answer this question now. However, while it is true that other terrorist groups have enjoyed this reality in the past[24], their pseudostate or close collaboration with official state authorities not only facilitates the planning and preparation of their attacks, training of foreign fighters before they are sent back home to stage attacks, but also their capacity to develop or acquire weapons of mass destruction more easily than before. Combined with their unwillingness to make any distinction between those that ought to be targeted, this feat makes contemporary terrorism a more serious threat than ever that cannot be ignored and needs to be fought in an effective and moral manner. This important topic will be discussed later in this book.

For the time being, I will solely emphasise the inherent risk of terrorism, leading to an erosion of the moral rules of warfare on the part of states being targeted by this type of violence (such as the resort to torture against these irregular fighters), the adoption of improper rules of engagement that can lead to the misuse of lethal technologies (Caron, 2019e, 2020a), and on the decay of the norms and values that define liberal states and Western democracies at the domestic level. As previously argued (2022ab), Western societies are now strongly organised around a 'Hobbesian understanding of life' in the sense that individuals view the state through the lens of their obligation to prevent them from dying (which has been clearly demonstrated during the COVID-19 pandemic where people massively supported their respective governments even if it meant introducing harsh liberticidal and disproportional measures that deprived them of their freedom). This is precisely when this logic prevails, as states have a tendency to overreact by trying to kill a mosquito with a bazooka, as they feel that they have failed at their primary mission. They indeed pass laws or impose decrees that result in the negation of what they are officially stand for, that is, freedom and rule of law. As Laqueur reminds us, the War on Terror has led Great Britain to reinforce the domestic surveillance of its citizens, thereby seriously eroding their right to privacy (2018, p. 89). There are indeed serious reasons to fear that these liberticidal measures will outlast the virus, as was rightfully stated by Edward Snowden, 'When we see emergency measures passed, particularly today, they tend to be sticky[25], or by Douglas Rutzen, who argued that while 'It's really easy to construct emergency powers, it's really difficult

---

24 The Assassins were for instance in control of a territory composed of various strongholds in Persia and Syria.

25 Thomas Macaulay, 'Snowden warns: The surveillance states we're creating now will outlast the virus'. https://thenextweb.com/neural/2020/03/25/snowden-warns-the-surveillance-states-were-creating-now-will-outlast-the-coronavirus/

to deconstruct them'[26]. The American Patriot Act provides a good example of this phenomenon. While it was initially designed as short-term legislation intended to help government agencies combat terrorism, this law has since been regularly renewed and has now become a common tool at the disposal of the US government for cases that are unrelated to anti-terrorist purposes (Caron, 2020b).

However, without wanting to minimise the impacts that this overreaction can have at the domestic level, this book focuses on the challenges associated with fighting terrorist threats at the global scale. However, before doing so, it is important to discuss guerrilla warfare and how it can be assessed from a moral standpoint.

---

26 Selam Gebrekidan, 'For Autocrats, and Others, Coronavirus Is a Chance to Grab Even More Power', New York Times, March 30, 2020. https://www.nytimes.com/2020/03/30/world/europe/coronavirus-governments-power.html

Chapter 2
Assessing the Morality of Guerrilla Warfare

In the previous chapter, I presented what I believe to be the best manner of defining terrorism, that is, the arbitrariness of its violence that deliberately targets individuals in an indiscriminate fashion. This type of violence, which can be used by both state and non-state actors, has been presented as different from the one associated with guerrilla groups whose way of operating is more discriminate and only directed at people who are thought to be the active perpetrators of evil[27]. Therefore, those who have been involved in what needs to be labelled as guerrilla warfare, such as Gerasim Romanenko, have very often claimed the 'purity of their methods' to be more ethical than those associated with mass revolution or terrorism (see Laqueur, 2004, p. 86). Thus, while the former individuals are compared with outlaws and criminals, the latter are more comparable with legitimate combatants, despite them not fully abiding by the customs of war (with the most important exception being those not wearing distinctive uniforms during their military operations). These two forms of violence are therefore fundamentally different because guerrilla warfare assumes that the civilian hinterland is part of the battlefield, while terrorism refuses to do so (Gross, 2006, p. 1). Further, while guerrilla tactics are performed according to the customary laws of warfare, terrorist acts are not. Thus assuming that guerrilla warfare and terrorism refer more or less to the same reality is inaccurate, because these two notions refer to very distinct realities[28].

Nevertheless, their willingness to abide by Albert Camus' idea that 'Even in destruction, there's a right way and a wrong way – and there are limits' (1958,

---

27 Which is why a definition of terrorism like the one given by Burleigh T. Wilkins is unable to distinguish terrorism from guerrilla warfare and ends up confusing in the same category the actions of bin Laden with the ones of WWII French *résistants:* 'Terrorism is the attempt to achieve political, social, economic, or religious change by the actual or threatened use of violence against persons or property; the violence employed in terrorism is aimed partly at destabilizing the existing political or social order, but mainly at publicizing the goals or cause espoused by the terrorists; often, though not always, terrorism is aimed at provoking extreme counter-measures which will win public support for the terrorists and their cause (...)' (1992, p. 6)

28 C.A.J. Coady is right in arguing the following: '(...) that we should continue to make a distinction between two broad types of revolutionary violence [one being "revolutionary violence" that refers to guerrilla warfare and the other one being "terrorism", that which is directed at what would be legitimate targets if the revolution were justified and that which is directed at non-combatants. We should reserve the term "terrorism" only for the latter and it can be unequivocally condemned' (1985, p. 65).

https://doi.org/10.1515/9783110757569-003

p. 258) should not automatically lead us to conclude that their actions are automatically morally acceptable. On the contrary, before doing so, it is first necessary to wonder what makes their targets legitimate targets against whom violent actions may be used. This is discussed in this chapter.

Similarly to terrorist organisations, guerrilla groups have historically fought for a variety of causes, and it is therefore impossible to limit this form of political violence to a sole fighting objective just like it is problematic, for example, to associate terrorism solely with religion. This type of insurgency is multi-faceted. However, their clear willingness not to deliberately harm innocent civilians transcends the diversity of causes guerrilla groups have fought for. Furthermore, as has been developed in the previous chapter, terrorist organisations that have also fought for various causes nonetheless all share the same strategy of indiscriminate killing.

Groups formed around a revolutionary agenda are one of the most well-known types of guerrilla insurgency. Having first appeared in the 19th century, these groups were driven by their opposition to capitalism and the need to provoke a revolution on the part of the proletariats. Considering the tremendous societal and economic changes that the United States and industrialised nations of Europe were going through at the time, it is unsurprising that these groups first emerged in the second half of the 19th century. The unprecedented technological progress of the time combined with the rapid rise of capitalism inevitably led to the enrichment of a few and impoverishment of many. This led to the creation of an anarcho[29]-socialist revolutionary political movement that was, for the most part, intellectual and political, but also violent. In this regard, Piotr Kropotkine was probably the first to openly advocate the need for violent actions through the use of 'propaganda by the deed' that aimed at waking up popular conscience through powerful acts. The primary targets of these actions were individuals who were identified either as the driving force of the oppression of the masses (capitalists) or those who were thought to be protecting them (government representatives). Therefore, French President Sadi Carnot was assassinated in 1894, Spanish Prime Minister Antonio Canovas in 1897, the Austro-Hungarian Empress Elizabeth (also known as Sissi) in 1898, King Umberto 1st of Italy in 1900, American President William McKingley in 1901, and attempts against Spanish King Alfonso XII in 1878 or Henry Clay Frick, French politicians Jules Ferry (in 1884) and

---

29 Although anarchism is usually associated with the destruction of the state, the main anarchist thinkers of the time—Pierre Joseph Proudhon and Piotr Kropotkine—had a reformist agenda in mind.

Leon Gambetta (in 1881), or of the director of the Carnegie Steel Company after he refused to increase the salary of his employees and after some of them were fired upon while they were occupying the company's factories.

However, history has probably remembered the Russian anarchists, especially members of organisations like the *Narodnaïa Volia* (which stands for 'People's Will'), as the quintessential case-study of this type of violent revolutionary socialism. Founded in 1879, the organisation's main goal was to prevent the growing liberal intelligentsia from fulfilling its plan to implement a more modern and democratic society in Russia which would have meant appropriation in the hands of the bourgeoisie the vast lands that were still the possession of the Russian state (more than half of them to be more precise), thereby simply replacing one form of workers tyranny by another. For the *Narodnovoltsi*, violent actions against the Tsar himself would trigger the necessary conditions for a popular revolution. 'Land and Liberty' became their motto. In the fall of 1879 and the following winter, members of *Narodnovoltsi* made numerous attempts at the Tsar's life by blowing up train convoys he was voyaging on board or at the Winter Palace in St. Petersburg before finally succeeding in 1881. The reaction of the authorities in the aftermath of this assassination eventually caused the group to collapse. Nonetheless, the revolutionary effort was carried on by other socialist and revolutionary groups who multiplied the assassinations of members of the Romanov royal family as well as high-ranked Russian statesmen. Importantly, many assassinations were perpetrated by individuals who declared themselves socialist revolutionaries despite not being members of the organisation. This situation resembles many contemporary terrorists who claim allegiance to Al Qaeda or ISIL without in many cases having established any relation with the organisations themselves. Although separated by almost a century, this type of guerrilla warfare also has similar aims and scope as the actions of the Red Army Faction that operated in West Germany mainly in the 1970s or the Italian Red Brigades during the same period that both fought capitalism.

Other important groups that have historically used guerrilla tactics are associated with what can be called 'national liberation' or 'secessionist' movements. This category includes contemporary groups, such as the Irish Republican Army (IRA), the Viet Minh in Indochina, the Basque ETA (*Euskadi Ta Askatasuna*), the *Front de libération du Québec* (FLQ), the Black Hand organisation dedicated to the union of all Serbs within the same entity and whose members killed the Austro-Hungarian Archduke Franz-Ferdinand and his wife in Sarajevo in 1914, and even some American revolutionaries in the early stages of the Revolution (Polk, 2008, pp. 11–12). As previously argued, owing to their numerical inferiority and lack of weaponry, almost all these groups have made a strategic decision to adopt irregular and elusive means of warfare to harass their enemies as much as possible and force them to give in. However, there are notable exceptions to this trend, and although some of these groups have initially resorted to guerrilla tactics, others have chosen to move from this type of insurgency to conventional warfare. In this regard, the Viet Minh is a good example. Alongside 33 other members of the organisation, Vo Nguyen Giap launched two surprise raids against French outposts in December 1944, similarly to what the IRA had done a few decades ago. After the end of WWII, the Viet Minh forces were able to regain their momentum after Mao took control of continental China and provided sheltered bases and heavy weapons to the Vietnamese, allowing them to benefit from weapons that allowed them to fight on an equal footing against the French. This explains why their guerrilla tactics evolved into a more conventional framework. We can also say the same about the 13 American Southern states that opted for secession in 1861 and who chose to mobilise a conventional army in their struggle against the Union rather than resorting to guerrilla tactics. Simultaneously, the move from irregular insurgency to conventional warfare was also associated with the wearing of distinctive uniforms by those fighting these groups. Their capacity to match the military strength of their respective enemy, and in some cases the disgust of military leaders for what they believed was an ungentlemanly way of fighting, made that choice obvious for both these groups. This was especially the case with George Washington, who had spent his entire career within the British military, did everything he could to transform the insurgents under his command into a European-like army which almost cost him victory (the Americans can indeed thank the French for providing enough support that ultimately allowed them to outmatch the British forces). Indeed, Washington believed that it was more noble and prestigious to fight in a conventional manner and his diaries were full of depreciating remarks about what became known a few years later as guerrilla tactics (Polk, 2008, p. 18).

Third, we could also add a separate category of guerrilla groups that can be labelled as 'resisting a foreign invasion'. Although national liberation or secessionist groups often claim to resist what they call the domination of a foreign state, the aforementioned examples are nonetheless distinct from the various movements of resistance that appeared in many European countries following their invasion by the Nazis or the Taliban-led insurrection in Afghanistan following the overthrow of their regime after 9/11, in the sense that they appeared many decades (even in some cases, many centuries) after their national territory was seized by a foreign power[30]. We may need to add the Sicarii to the category of

---

30 For instance, although French Canada was conquered by the British in 1763, the FLQ started

national liberation/secessionist movements, who started their operations against the Romans some 60 years after their territory had fallen under their occupation. In addition, similarly to the above-mentioned groups, some of these groups also moved from irregular insurgency by becoming a conventional force that operated as such when their strengths matched those of their enemies. In this regard, the case of Tito's partisans in Yugoslavia who first resorted to guerrilla tactics can be mentioned as they eventually evolved into a conventional force comprising no less than 650,000 combatants forming more than 50 divisions[31].

Despite their different reasons for taking up arms, all these groups are nonetheless related regarding their preferred means of fighting. Whether for moral or strategic reasons, they emphasise on solely targeting individuals who they thought had lost immunity against death because of their central political or social role rather than resorting to indiscriminate means of warfare. As previously argued, this was the case with the Jewish Sicarii, who are known today as one of the first groups to use terror to achieve a political objective in an organised way, and took great pains to determine who was to be targeted. This was also true for Russian anarchists, and notably the early days of the Irish Republican Army (IRA), whose members purposefully targeted active representatives of the British state who were considered as combatants (a more thorough discussion about this status will follow in the upcoming pages). For instance, on the eve of Easter 1920, the IRA launched more than 300 attacks against police stations and killed 11 individuals working for British secret services a few months later. Under Michael Collins' leadership, members of the IRA were sent to Liverpool, where they killed two members of a counter-terrorism unit. In Italy, the Red Brigades followed the same pattern by targeting individuals who incarnated the symbols of capitalism in their eyes. To shake up the working class, its members went on strike against multinational corporations by kidnapping the CEO of Fiat in 1972, a director of Alfa Romeo, another director from Fiat a year later and, more famously, Aldo Moro, the Italian Prime Minister.

As previously argued, it is important to highlight that not all these groups resorted to guerrilla tactics. Thus, it would be a mistake to associate groups fighting for the establishment of a socialist revolution, secession, national liberation, or resistance solely with guerrilla warfare, just like it would be a mistake to associate religion with terrorism. For instance, although apocalyptic religious be-

---

its operations only in the early 1960s. The same can be said with the Irish case or with the Basques.

31 As journalist Basil Davidson wrote: 'By the middle of 1943 partisan resistance to the Germans and their allies had grown from the dimensions of a mere nuisance to those of a major factor in the general situation'

liefs have usually led to terrorism over guerrilla tactics, there also exist groups whose insurgency was primarily a religious one that nonetheless chose the latter path. For example, the Ismaili chose to strike discriminately against selected individuals who they thought were legitimate targets, such as Nizam al-Mulk. Subsequent murders included that of Conrad of Montferrat, King of Jerusalem, in 1192.

In return, there are also examples of groups that fit into the aforementioned categories that nonetheless chose to resort to terrorist means of fighting, such as Émile Henry, who detonated a bomb in February 1894 in a café next to the Saint-Lazare train station in Paris. In his final declaration, he said that because the authorities on the part of the state authorities resorted to mass and indiscriminate measures against anyone suspected of anarchist sympathies, the anarchists were also justified in striking indiscriminately (Gazette des Tribunaux, 29 April 1894, p. 419).

In other words, history has shown us that the same cause was fought through means associated with both guerrilla and terrorist tactics which has only confused people and analysts about this type of violence and has facilitated states' efforts to demonise the individuals involved in these groups. Consequently, there is no direct correlation between reasons for which insurgent groups are fighting and guerrilla or terrorist tactics, which is why it would be problematic to assess the moral legitimacy of guerrilla warfare and terrorism based on the cause of the groups that have chosen these two types of irregular warfare.

War is known for its ability to justify what is considered a crime in normal times, that is, killing other human beings. Consequently, just war theorists have attempted to justify this in numerous ways to absolve soldiers of murder. Thus, being able to provide a morally acceptable view of justified killing is of the outmost importance. This is precisely where terrorism has failed by refusing to adopt such a viewpoint and why their political violence is so heinous and inacceptable because it ends up killing and maiming victims who are unable to understand why they have targeted rather than somebody else who may simply have been walking on the other side of the street or on board a different plane when the attack was perpetrated.

The unwillingness of terrorist organisations to distinguish between legitimate and illegitimate targets is visible through their indiscriminate attacks and through the official rhetoric and writings of those leading them. Contrary to guerrilla groups that are prone to attribute guilt to a selected group of individuals who are therefore thought to have lost their immunity against harm, terrorist logic embraces an overly generous conception of collective responsibility that can only lead to a strategy of indiscriminate killing. They have historically assessed people's responsibility through two approaches: either by their simple involuntary and *de facto* membership in a group (this approach relies on the premise that responsibility is independent of individuals' choices), or because of the specific decisions they have made as members of the group (a responsibility that is therefore dependent on the choices of individuals). Even if the latter approach is thought to adopt a more restrictive view of collective responsibility, it can nonetheless fall short of providing a framework that can allow us to distinguish between those who ought to lose immunity and those who should not as I will explain later in this chapter.

In the first case, all individuals are understood as legitimate targets simply by virtue of their belonging to a group considered an enemy. Following this view, if all Israelis are thought to be responsible for the harm caused by their state to the Palestinian people, the latter therefore have a right to directly and intentionally target all Israelis with deadly violence. Accordingly, harming or killing women and children (or athletes, like those killed during the 1972 Olympic Games in Munich) will not be considered wrong in their eyes, as they will not be considered innocent, but as sharing a part of the blame for their governments' actions[32]. However, as the weaker conception of personal responsibility rests upon the idea that individuals are liable to lose immunity against harm and death based on their choices, it tends to limit the identity of those who are thought to be legitimate targets. It is this latter view that has been privileged by guerrilla groups. However, this does not necessarily justify their violence from a moral standpoint as this assessment of personal responsibility can prove itself as indiscriminate as the previous one, as Bin Laden's case proves.

Both approaches were used by Laden to justify his terrorist actions[33]. Al Qaeda's leader once argued that on the basis of people being American or citizens of states supporting U.S. policies, he supported the view that this criterion was sufficient to justify resorting to violence against them. This was clear in the *fatwa* he issued in 1998 in which he wrote:

---

[32] Seumas Miller summarizes this perspective in the following manner: 'According to the morality of collective identity, the members of some oppressor or enemy group are guilty purely by virtue of membership of that national, racial, ethnic or religious group. So a white South African who opposed apartheid, was nevertheless, guilty in the eyes of the extremist anti-apartheid groups simply by virtue of being white. All Americans are guilty of oppressing Muslims simply by virtue of being American citizens, according to some extremist Al Qaeda pronouncements. (...) A person is a wrongdoer—and thus liable to lethal attack by way of response—not by virtue of what he or she as an individual has deliberately done, but rather by virtue of (more or less) unchosen aspects of his or her collective identity' (2009, p. 61).

[33] In this case, the word 'terrorism' adequately describes his actions rather than 'guerrilla' because of the indiscriminate nature of his violence.

> The ruling to kill the Americans and their allies—civilians and military—is an individual duty for every Muslim who can do it in any country in which it is possible to do it, in order to liberate the al-Aqsa Mosque and the holy mosque [Mecca] from their grip, and in order for their armies to move out of all the lands of Islam, defeated and unable to threaten any Muslim. This is in accordance with the words of Almighty Allah, "and fight the pagans all together as they fight you all together", and "fight them until there is no more tumult or oppression, and there prevail justice and faith in Allah" (quoted in Laqueur, 2004, p. 412).

Knowing that religious denomination is often not a personal choice but rather a decision imposed by one's parents, it would make sense to consider this justification for killing under the lens of a strong view of personal responsibility that lies upon their unchosen belonging to a specific group. Furthermore, because Islamist terrorist organisations consider all Westerners as *de facto* 'disbelievers' (that is, either Christians or Jewish), it is challenging to consider this justification for killing as a matter of choice. Such reasoning can also be found in the *Practical Course for Guerrilla War* written by Abd Al-'Aziz Al-Muqrin, the former Al Qaeda leader in the Arabian Peninsula. Although it bears many similarities with the IRA's Green Book or the tactics advocated by Carlos Marighela regarding the main objective of what ought to be Al Qaeda's fight against its enemies (to prolong the war to slowly wear out the enemy's will to fight), the phases of guerrilla warfare (which are in this regard very similar to those once advocated by Mao), and what tactics to employ. This document nonetheless advocates for a strong conception of responsibility and, consequently, is another reason that makes it impossible to associate Al Qaeda with the previously mentioned guerrilla groups. More precisely, the manual calls on all Muslims to 'kill Jews and Christians' and to 'turn their countries into a living hell' by targeting in order of priority the 'citizens of infidel countries directly involved in supporting the local apostates' (quoted in Cigar, 2009, p. 129)[34]. This manner of considering personal responsibility is also at the core of ISIL's violence and highlights the problematic mix between religious views and the simple fact of living in a Western society. For instance, the organisation spokesperson Abu Muhammad al-Adnani said the following in 2014:

> (...) do not let this battle pass you by wherever you may be. You must strike the soldiers, patrons, and troops of the tawâghît. Strike their police, security, and intelligence members, as well as their treacherous agents. Destroy their beds. Embitter their lives for them and

---

34 More precisely, Jews (with the priority given to the Jews of American and Israel) then Christians (in the following priority: from the United States, Great Britain, Spain, Australia, Canada and Italy).

busy them with themselves. If you can kill a disbelieving American or European—especially the spiteful and filthy French—or an Australian, or a Canadian, or any other disbeliever from the disbelievers waging war, including the citizens of the countries that entered into a coalition against the Islamic State, then rely upon Allah, and kill him in any manner or way however it may be. Do not ask for anyone's advice and do not seek anyone's verdict. Kill the disbeliever whether he is a civilian or military, for they have the same ruling. Both of them are disbelievers. Both of them are considered to be waging war [the civilian by belonging to a state waging war against the Muslims]. Both of their blood and wealth is legal for you to destroy, for blood does not become illegal or legal to spill, and the military uniform does not make blood legal to spill. The only things that make blood illegal and legal to spill are Islam and a covenant (peace treaty, dhimmi [contract], etc.]. Blood becomes legal to spill through disbelief. So whoever is a Muslim, his blood and wealth are sanctified. And whoever is a disbeliever, his wealth is legal for a Muslim to take, and his blood is legal to spill. His blood is like the blood of a dog (...) (quoted in Ingram et al., 2020, pp. 184–185).

In a manner reminiscent of Karl Jaspers' category of political guilt (which will be discussed at length in the fifth chapter), Bin Laden also justified his actions through a weaker version of responsibility following the 9/11 attacks that nonetheless resulted in a justification for indiscriminate killings. He said:

> The American people should remember that they pay taxes to their government and that they voted for their president. Their government makes weapons and provides them to Israel, which they use to kill Palestinian Muslims. Given that the American Congress is a committee that represents the people, the fact that it agrees with the actions of the American government proves that America in its entirety is responsible for the atrocities that it is committing against Muslims (2005, pp. 140–141).

Such a justification, which gives *carte blanche* to mass indiscriminate murders, is problematic for several reasons, and is an ideology with no basis from the standpoint of collective or individual moral responsibility (Miller, 2009, p. 61). First, in such terrorist attacks, there are high chances that individuals who do not satisfy the terrorists' criteria of collective responsibility might be harmed or killed. In this regard, we can think of children as well as individuals who may not benefit from what terrorists call an oppressive system, or those who are also actively opposed to their country's policy. For instance, when Émile Henry threw the bomb in Café Terminus in 1894, the place was not filled entirely with bourgeois people; underpaid members of the working class, such as waiters and cooks, were also present. The same can be said when a bomb blows up in a bus or train in New York, London, or Madrid. People who vote for candidates opposed to what terrorists see as unlawful policies might also be harmed or killed by these attacks. Additionally, terrorists may argue that despite their opposition, they nonetheless benefit from such policies, which is enough to make them guilty as accomplices to the crimes of their state. However, this argument is flawed. Indeed, we need to consider that many of these people are simply unable to emigrate to a country that is better aligned with their beliefs. Moreover, for authoritarian/totalitarian states, we cannot ignore that being actively opposed to one's state policy always has terrible consequences. Thus, it is worth wondering if it is fair to criticise them for their silence and passivity, knowing that dissidence on their part might result in their death. Such a conception of collective responsibility would be a major drift away from the current rules of warfare, as it would lead us to ignore all distinctions during wartime, an idea put forward during the 1990–1991 Gulf War by some members of the US Air Force (Draper, 1998). In one briefing, a senior member of this branch of the military said that the Iraqi people could be targeted because they refused to exercise control over their state's policy and did nothing to undermine their government after it invaded Kuwait. Such an assessment of collective responsibility would be like assigning liability to all employees working in a company that produces a life-threatening product, such as a tobacco company or one that produces pesticides. This broad and indiscriminate understanding of responsibility is, dangerous and, if applied, would lead to total barbarianism as it would allow the killing of everyone during wartime.

However, although bin Laden's actions were characterised by total indiscrimination, it would nonetheless be a mistake to conclude that the whole jihadist ideology is monolithic in this regard. Indeed, the main inspiration for today's jihadists comes from the 13th century theologian Ibn Taymiyyah, whose works are still quoted by virtually every radical Islamist and who explicitly called on his followers to exert a sense of discrimination when striking against their enemies. He wrote:

> Since lawful warfare is essentially jihad and since its aim is that the religion is Allah entirely and Allah's word is uppermost, therefore, according to all Muslims, those who stand in the way of this aim must be fought. As for those who cannot offer resistance or cannot fight, such as women, children, monks, old people, the blind, handicapped and the like, they shall not be killed, unless they actually fight with words [e.g. by propaganda] and acts [e.g. by spying or otherwise assisting in the warfare]. Some [jurists] are of the opinion that they are unbelievers, but they make an exception for women and children since they constitute property for Muslims. However, the first opinion is the correct one, because we may only fight those who fight us when we want to make Allah's religion victorious. Allah, Who is exalted, has said in this respect: "And fight in the way of Allah those who fight you, but transgress not: Allah loves not the transgressors" (quoted in Lacqueur, 2004, p. 393).

In return, guerrilla groups (similarly to what was advocated by Ibn Taymiyyah) refused to adopt a strong view of personal responsibility and privileged a narrower and more exclusive view of this matter. It is this ethics that makes them —at least in theory—lawful combatants, despite the irregular nature of their fight. Although I will expound on this further in the following pages, I believe that dismissing unethical, irregular types of warfare simply because they are not fought by state entities is problematic and would prevent any stateless group from resorting to legitimate violence when they face a type of oppression that leaves them no other choice. I feel this is partly why guerrilla groups, contrary to terrorists, have been able to generate a form of respect and admiration on the part of intellectuals[35]. A heroic resistance to what is perceived as a genuine oppression through the targeting of people who have sometimes themselves recognised that they were legitimate targets, such as Italian King Umberto 1st who recognised after an unsuccessful attack against his life that 'this kind of risk is part of the job' (Primoratz, 2013, p. 17).

Guerrilla groups have often suggested a thorough analysis of who ought to be targeted with violent actions its reasons. The best example is probably that of Russian radical socialist Sergey Nechayev, famously known for his *Cathechism of the Revolutionist* written in 1869, in which he determined categories of people against whom violent actions were thought to be justified. However, despite his efforts to establish a manner of discriminating between legitimate targets and to determine the priority of who ought to be targeted, Nechayev's manifesto remained highly problematic, as it did not rely on a weak conception of personal responsibility. Rather, it decided to solely consider the positive consequences that their death would have on the progress of the revolutionary cause. Points 15 and 16 of his manifesto are clear in this regard:

> 15. All of this foul society must be split up into several categories: the first category comprises those to be condemned immediately to death. The society should compile a list of these condemned persons in order of the relative harm they may do to the successful progress of the revolutionary cause, and thus in order of their removal;
>
> 16. In compiling these lists and deciding the order referred to above, the guiding principle must not be the individual acts of villainy committed. By the person, nor even by the hatred he provokes among the society or the people. This villainy and hatred, however, may to a certain extent be useful, since they help to incite popular rebellion. The guiding principle must be the measure of service the person's death will necessarily render to the revolutionary cause. Therefore, in the first instance all those must be annihilated who are especially harmful to the revolutionary organization, and whose sudden and violent deaths will also inspire the greatest fear in the government and, by depriving it of its cleverest and most energetic figures, will shatter its strength (quoted in Laqueur, 2004, pp. 73–74).

---

35 In this regard, we can mention Modern authors like Émile Zola or Stéphane Mallarmé who talked about the 'eternal black poetry' of anarchists and 'decorative blast' of dynamite, respectively (Chaliand & Blin, 2015, p. 151), and Ancient thinkers according to whom killing tyrants was a noble gesture worthy of respect.

If we are to find proper ways from a moral standpoint to distinguish between who ought to be the legitimate and illegitimate targets of the political violence of guerrilla groups, we must start with the oldest and most selective form of targeted killing, that is, tyrannicide, which is probably as old as philosophy itself. Plato and Aristotle were both renowned for perceiving tyranny as an impure form of government because of the regime's inability to implement justice. As this regime was thought to deprive individuals of their freedom by allowing a single individual to abuse his power to serve his own selfish interests, the murderers of tyrants—not to be confused with those called 'monarchs' who were, contrary to tyrants, able to privilege the common interest—a noble action (as claimed by Cicero) that even justified in their eyes a recompense as Lucian of Samasota wrote (quoted in Laqueur, 2004, p. 17). Other thinkers followed the same path. For instance, John of Salisbury wrote that it was a matter of justice that tyrants ought to be killed. The logic that transcended most of them was that being a single ruler was not, in itself, a justified reason to resort to violence, thereby eliminating the claim that tyrannicide lies upon a strong conception of personal responsibility. Rather, the logic was permitted only when a certain threshold of vices and licentiousness that made him act beyond the laws of honour and decency (such as, in the words of Juan de Mariana, his actions that are destroying the state, the confiscation of public and private fortunes as his or his contempt for religion[36]) was crossed and when no other option was possible. In this regard, Thomas of Aquinas saw three non-violent courses of action: 1) to constitute monarchy in a way that would allow the people to depose such an unvirtuous ruler; 2) when an appeal to a higher authority is possible (such as the Pope) to depose the tyrant; and 3) to pray to God in the hope that he moves the monarch's heart and convinces him to confess his sins.

Evidently, tyrannicide has historically been justified on two important premises. First, this type of assassination lies upon a weak conception of authority and rather than justifying the murder of a sovereign on the basis of his political authority does so on his own chosen decision to drift into an unvirtuous licence and in the oppression of his people. In this case, there is no difference in whether the sovereign has reached his office alone or through bloodline transmission. In the latter case, although his political status was not the outcome of his own choice, the same cannot be said regarding his lack of virtue. Second, the decision

---

36 For his part, Thomas of Aquinas thought that this red line was crossed when the tyrant was becoming '(...) a violent ruler. More comparable to a wild animal than a human being, who panders entirely to his own passions, sows discord among his subjects, drives them into poverty and degradation, and in short reduces them to the level of slaves' (quoted in Laqueur, 2004, p. 28).

to kill this unvirtuous ruler ought to be taken as a last resort when no other choices that might halt his tyranny are available to people.

Furthermore, there is ground to argue that people who have voluntarily engaged on the path of tyranny must share the moral responsibility of their actions, which can ultimately take the form of their assassination. When a certain threshold of inadmissibility is reached, targeting them, therefore, should not be considered a terrorist act because the target has committed actions that have led him to lose his immunity against death (Nathanson, 2010, pp. 42–43). This was clearly the reason behind *Narodnaïa Volia*'s decision to kill Tsar Alexander II, who had to bear personal responsibility for the brutal repression, plight of the peasantry, reaction in the field of education, and domestic politics, as an unrestricted monarch.

If such an individual is deemed to have lost his moral innocence because of his tyranny, insurgents have argued that the same logical fate awaits those who are making this tyranny possible by implementing it actively. Additionally, insurgents have used their direct role in either creating or implementing unjust policies as grounds to deny their immunity against death[37]. In this view, Alex P. Schmid has argued that individuals who have taken up leadership roles as statesmen or direct instruments for the implementation of state policies, ought to know that they are party to an unjust system of government and, as such, attacks against their lives should not come as a surprise, even when unexpected. In return, the logic is that individuals who do not play any direct role in this system ought to retain their immunity against harm and death, which would include the family members of the tyrant and his accomplices (1992). For argument's sake, if we consider that Grand Duke Sergei, who was assassinated in 1905 by Russian radical socialists, had lost his moral innocence because of his direct involvement in the regime, this was not true for his wife or nephews who were sitting with him in his carriage two days prior to his assassination which is why the attackers chose to call off the attack. Assuming that these individuals would have been guilty by association because of their filial relationship with the one who had lost immunity against harm and death, would mean resorting to an immoral logic of strong personal responsibility.

As Gérard Chaliand and Arnaud Blin have argued, these examples show that guerrilla fighters are clearly animated by a type of ethics of personal responsibility—in its weak form—that, when applied in a restrictive fashion (unlike in the

---

37 Although not all the time. Plutarch indeed reminds us that Brutus opposed the killing of Mark Anthony (described as a lawless man opposed to the republican principle) alongside the one of Caesar.

way bin Laden has done), justifies the targeting of a handful of individuals for their involvement in an immoral regime. Unlike criminals, these murderers abide by ethical principles that aim to limit as much harm and violence as possible, a feature that shares many similarities with how states justify their own resort to violence (2015, pp. 227–228). In this sense, and because I do not see why state entities should automatically enjoy moral superiority over non-state entities in terms of the legitimate use of violence, guerrilla fighters should be considered legitimate combatants (yet, fighting in an irregular manner because of the tremendous asymmetric disadvantages they face in terms of means at their disposal). However, given that guerrilla organisations are willing to distinguish between legitimate and illegitimate targets does not necessarily justify their killings from a moral perspective. Two important questions must be addressed in this regard. First, is their view of personal responsibility too generous, and second, does even the most restrictive view of personal responsibility permit guerrilla groups to resort to lethal actions against their enemies?

Even though guerrilla groups respect a moral code of conduct very close to the rules of warfare, this does not automatically justify their violent actions from a moral perspective. Resorting to lethal actions against other human beings must be grounded in solid moral justifications. This means that some guerrilla groups' assassinations will be justified, while others will not. How can we conduct this assessment? If we return to the aforementioned discussion on tyranny, we must admit that the killing of these corrupted monarchs has been historically justified on numerous grounds including their unwillingness to govern in favour of the common good of the multitude but rather to privilege their private interests to a point of denying freedom to their people by enslaving them, for their infringements of the laws of God, or even for opposing the unification of Italy (which was the case for Vittorio Alfieri). This begs the question of whether denying people of their freedom ought to bear the same consequences than opposing the laws of God. This can obviously lead to relativism in a world divided by numerous competing religions—or a specific political project—whether independence or for the sake of a socialist revolution.

The starting point of this discussion ought to be the idea that resistance against oppression is justifiable when a state violates human rights (Finlay, 2015; Buchanan, 2013; Iser, 2017; Gross, 2015). However, the degree of resistance will take different forms depending on the nature of oppression. More precisely, the means by which individuals or groups who are victims of oppression can legitimately defend and protect their natural rights will follow a spectrum that ranges from non-violent measures to armed resistance. This is because despite being a catch-all notion, oppression must be assessed based on objective criteria. Otherwise, all forms of oppression—whether individuals living under a tyranny, nations denied their right to self-determine freely, the economic domination of the bourgeois claimed by leftist groups, or the cultural hegemony of a so-called imperialist culture—will be considered to have the same meaning and will, consequently, justify the use of violent and lethal means of action. Adopting such an expansive view of armed resistance through guerrilla warfare would be problematic as it would justify resorting to lethal actions for members of national minorities denied their right to speak their language or practice their religion, and individuals who live under a genocidal regime that can order their death without warning at any time.

These actual or foreseeable threats must be institutionalised and not the result of violations of individuals' rights by low-level rogue agents of the state. Unfortunately, such actions will almost always happen in societies, and the misdemeanour of one police officer or soldier cannot alter the nature of a regime that allows dissent and its citizens' right to fight oppression—be it cultural, religious, or economic—through democratic means. In such circumstances, we would be unable to talk about violently oppressive or repressive regimes and, consequently, would not justify the resort to violent actions on the part of victims of this violation.

The right to kill can only be justified in cases of self-defence, that is, when individuals' lives are under immediate institutionalised threat or they are facing a credible threat against their lives or limbs. Undoubtedly, the situation experienced by Jews during WWII is probably the quintessential example of this scenario, and individuals whose lives are at the mercy of an immoral and murderous force. In the latter case, we might think of WWII *résistants* who fought the Nazis after their countries had been invaded by Hitler's forces, as well as the people who opposed the tyrannical rule of Muhammar Gaddafi in 2011. In this case, Libyan dictator's opposition was grounded on the deadly threats he made against the protesters[38], and him displaying the capacity and intention to fulfil his menace and a history of brutal reprisal of opponents that exacerbated the credibility of his menaces[39]. Arguably, once this threshold has been reached, the resort to guerrilla tactics is justified insofar as—and this will recall Thomas of Aquinas's three aforementioned conditions—there are no other valuable non-violent options to halt this situation. In my view, the following three realities must be considered. First, the political nature of the regime in which guerrilla groups are operating. When individuals like Hitler or Gaddafi expose others

---

38 After calling them 'cockroaches', Gaddafi said his opponents would be shown no mercy ('Any Libyan who takes arms against Libya will be executed').
39 The 1996 massacre at the Abu Salim prison is a good example in this regard.

to such cruelty, it goes without saying that they wave their right not to be themselves terrorised. For example, bank robbers who hold people hostages at gunpoint while their partners empty the safe, their decision to deny others their right to life can only result in them losing their own immunity against being killed. Indeed, it is not morally reprehensible to do everything we can to stop someone whose actions pose a direct threat to our life. A genuine right of self-defence —as is the case in the aforementioned circumstances—clearly overrides the perpetrator's right not to be harmed. In such cases, violence can rightfully be met with violence.

However, contrary to oppressive or repressive regimes that pose an actual or predictable threat to individuals' freedom, lives, or limbs if they are to protest or ask for a change in policy, states that allow expression of the frustrations of those who claim to be suffering from forms of oppression have alternatives other than resorting to lethal force. The case of the British rule in Ireland before the scission of the island is a good example in this regard. As Christopher Finlay wrote:

> (...) in the late nineteenth and early twentieth century, Britain afforded opportunities to the nationalists of the Irish Parliamentary Party to pursue their political goals through representatives at Westminster who, in turn, promoted their agenda by negotiation with other British parties. This resulted after some decades of agitation in the Third Home Rule Bill, which (unlike its two predecessors) passed successfully through the Houses of Parliament to enter the statute books in September 1914. The Bill did not, by any means, represent the complete fulfilment of the more robust aspirations of some Irish nationalists, but it went some way in their direction and could, perhaps, have provided a basis for further progress in time had the agenda of parliamentary nationalists not been overtaken by separatist proponents of armed force with the Easter Rising in 1916 and the later War of Independence (1919–21). (...) Even assuming that British rule could reasonably be seen as oppressive, the resort to force in these circumstances lacked the necessary prima facie justification since Irish subjects were not by that time subject to Life and Limb Rights violations and those mobilized behind the Irish Parliamentary Party were not subject to Life and Limb Rights violations (2015, p. 83).

Indeed, achieving Ireland's independence through non-violent means might have taken more time than the guerrilla strategy that was mainly designed by Michael Collins, but that option was nonetheless a viable one. Consequently, although he and his men discriminately targeted those who were thought to have lost their immunity against harm and death, there are grounds to believe that violence was not the last resort at the disposal of the Irish and, accordingly, makes the IRA's lethal actions immoral and unjustified following the logic I have presented so far. The same can be said with the actions of the *Front de libération du Québec* that culminated in 1970 when they kidnapped a British diplomat and Quebec's Minister of Justice (who later died[40] while being under the custody of four of its members) led the Canadian government to impose the War Measures Act. However, only six years after these events, an independentist party–the Parti Québécois– managed to take power in Quebec following a democratic election and organized a referendum on the province's independence four years later. This proves that violence was not a last resort in their case, as their pursued objective was clearly possible through the peaceful democratic process.

Second, the moral identity of those against whom our struggle is directed also plays a major role in justifying resorting to and refraining from lethal actions. Indians and Gandhi proved very well how non-violent resistance against British rule proved to be a highly-effective method for them to achieve their political objective of independence. When the enemy is a 'moral enemy', opponents have a wide range of non-violent leverages at their disposal, which is not necessarily the case against an 'immoral enemy' that is simply unmoved by the pleas of its opponents. Consequently, it makes it impossible for the victims of its inhumane tyranny to generate any leverage that might force the regime to alter its course of action. Therefore, non-violent options, namely non-cooperation with the enemy, are seen as tactically effective against a moral enemy, but not against one whose brutality takes precedence over any moral consideration. The identity of one's enemy ought to play a fundamental role in our assessment of non-violent options, as philosopher Jan Narveson reminded us:

> (...) it is worthwhile to point out that the general history of the human race certainly offers no support for the supposition that turning the other cheek always produces good effects on the aggressor. Some aggressors, such as the Nazis, were apparently just "egged on" by the "pacifist" attitude of their victims. Some of the S.S. men apparently became curious to see just how much torture the victim would put up with before he began to resist. Furthermore, there is the possibility that, while pacifism might work against some people (one might cite the British, against whom pacifism in India was apparently rather successful –but the British are comparatively nice people), it might fail against others (e.g. the Nazis) (1965, p. 263).

In a certain way, we might doubt whether guerrilla warfare can be justified within liberal democracies. Indeed, by allowing the expression of discontent—whether it refers to the economic struggle of the working class or the demands of national groups that seek political autonomy—these states are open to discussing

---

40 It is still unknown if he was executed by members of the organization or if he died from self-inflicted wounds caused by the shattered glass of the window he tried to escape from.

such matters, and history has shown us that, although it may only be achieved in the long run, they have found solutions to accommodate these grievances.

The third condition that might determine whether victims of human rights violations have a moral right to resort to violence is whether they can exert pressure on their enemies using effective external pressure—also referred to in the literature as 'regime certification/decertification"[41] (McAdam et al, 2001). Nowadays, most countries are not cut off from the outside world that has become more interdependent than ever before. This feature affects democracies as much as authoritarian regimes when their people have grievances. However, the chances of success of these protests will not necessarily depend on the degree of political indignation of people or the merits of their claim, but rather on whether their members are able to seize specific structural political opportunities. As is evident from other circumstances, one of the key factors (alongside the elite divide) is a regime's capacity to retain certification by external authorities. When it can do so, it has the capacity to prevent itself from being the victim of the political or economic consequences that can follow a violent reaction against those protesting, while the survival of an authoritarian rule that is vulnerable to decertification on the part of its allies is clearly at stake. In such a case, these regimes are left only with the option of being overthrown by their opponents or to make concessions. The leverage at the disposal of opposing groups is therefore huge. Many previous examples have tended to prove this claim. For instance, following the violent protests that shook Burma in the 1980s that nonetheless failed to overthrow the military junta that had assumed control in 1962 following a successful coup by general Ne Win, the regime's capacity to retain the support of its closest allies played a major role in its survival and willingness to resort to violence against its opponents. As Burma lacked dependence on a foreign state due to its largely autarkic economic policy, other countries were not in a position to effectively pressure its government for political change. In fact, while Thailand did not hesitate to arrest and deport back to Burma dissidents, other countries such as Singapore, China, and Pakistan kept selling arms to the junta, and Japan refused to boycott economic trade with the country (Schock 1999; Caron & Malikova, 2021). From this perspective, when groups have the capacity to force a regime's decertification because of its abuse of human rights or violence against its opponents, resorting to violent actions—even the most discriminate actions associated with guerrilla warfare—is therefore not a last resort. This is obviously

---

41 Certification can be defined as 'the validation of actors, their performances, and their claims by external authorities', while decertification refers to 'the withdrawal of such validation by key certifying agents' (McAdam et al. 2001, 204).

different for groups that are operating in countries that are impervious to the risk of being decertified.

In a way, this manner of justifying resorting to violence shares many similarities with the *jus ad bellum* logic that rests upon the idea that lethal actions are only acceptable when all other non-violent alternatives to war have have proved themselves to be ineffective. The reasons why this ought to be the case are easy to understand. In both cases, people's life immunity is at stake and being the primary natural right upon which the enjoyment of all others depends; it is necessary to ensure that denying some individuals their right to live is entirely justified and the only solution available. Therefore, any justification in this sense would need to meet the last-resort criterion. Furthermore, their willingness to abide by clear ethics of discrimination insufficient to justify their resort to violence from a moral standpoint. However, determining when guerrilla warfare is morally defendable is only one aspect of this equation. Another question is the identity of those who ought to be legitimately targeted. Again, this is a challenging issue.

Based on what has been said previously, individuals who are directly involved in the oppression and violation of other people's human rights can be deemed to have lost their life immunity when all other options to stop their crimes have failed or have no chance of succeeding. However, what does 'directly involved' mean more precisely? This notion refers primarily to individuals who have a genuine capacity to determine the denounced course of action and whose voice is required to implement it (when necessary), namely, members of the executive and legislative branches. Notably, assigning this type of responsibility is not revolutionary in itself, as individuals who are part of these branches of power in a country involved in violations of international norms are already targeted by non-violent forms of deterrence for backing up these unlawful practices. For instance, this has been the case in February 2022 with the 351 members of the Russian parliament, the Duma, who voted in favour of the recognition of independence of the Donetsk and Luhansk republics and who were sanctioned by the European Union. More specifically, those without whom unjust policies would not be able to exist in the first place must be aware that their personal responsibility is at stake. Even if their vote may have been coerced in some form (whether the obligation to abide by the party line at the risk of being expelled from it, being prevented from renewing one's electoral mandate, or being dismissed from one's position in the government), it is assumed that members of parliament and executive branch sought or have accepted these offices on their own will and have the possibility to resign from them whenever they wish to (or, in the worst-case scenario, to seek political asylum). As was the case with Hitler's cabinet members who were trialled at the Nuremberg trial in 1945–1946, those whose participation was instrumental to the *Führer*'s warmongering lunacy were thought to have engaged their personal responsibility in crimes against peace and were accordingly found guilty. This was also the case with German military high command members who were in a position to shape or influence their state's unlawful policy. For example, Field Marshall Wilhelm Keitel, who, alongside his position in the military, was also given significant policy-making powers. For instance, the Secret Defense Law of 1938 provided for a Plenipotentiary for Economy, whose task was to 'put all economic forces into the service of the Reich defense, and to safeguard economically the life of the German nation', and for a Plenipotentiary for Administration, whose duties were to take over 'the uniform leadership of the non-military administration with exception of the economic administration' upon the declaration of a 'state of defense'. Certain ministries were bound by the directives of the plenipotentiaries in peacetime. The latter were bound, in turn, under certain conditions, together with the ministries subordinate to them, to take directions from the Chief of the OKW [whose commander was Keitel himself]. Keitel could also, in a state of defense, issue orders to the Minister of Transport and Minister of Posts. In addition, he presided over the Council's Working Committee, which prepared the Council's decisions, saw that they were executed, and obtained collaboration between the armed forces, chief Reich offices, and the Party. Keitel regulated the this committee's activities and issued directions to the plenipotentiaries and certain Reich ministries to ensure the uniform execution of the council's decisions (Caron, 2018).

This logic also applies to rulers who have inherited power through the grace of birth. Although their accession to power may not have been their decision, the decision to implement or pursue an unjust policy remained their own. Therefore, those who play a direct role in the implementation of a great injustice, suffering, or the violation of basic moral rights, such as other people's right to life, not to be physically or psychologically damaged, not to be raped, or to be protected from grievous bodily harm are engaging their personal responsibility in the weak sense of the term: a responsibility that does not extend to their family members who do not play a similar direct role in the establishment or the execution of the unjust policy (Primoratz, 2013, p. 17; Shue, 1996; see also Taylor Wilkins, 1992, p. 96).

However, what about rulers who have acquired power through birth that remains largely symbolic, namely monarchs in parliamentary democracies? Although in theory, they still possess a tremendous amount of power, they are essentially left out of the decision-making process and are mainly mere figureheads, like the late Queen Elizabeth II. In the case of Great Britain, while it is true that no law can enter in effect without the monarch official approval (the royal sanction), it remains the UK head of state choice to oppose signing a law does not exist in our democratic era. Thus, is the monarch—and all her counterparts worldwide—a legitimate target? Again, this is not an easy question to answer. There are two possible methods to address this challenge. On the one hand, we could argue that these monarchs still have the possibility to resign from their position when they are bound to officially sanction an unjust policy as a sign of protest and opposition against it to not become an accomplice to a crime that might jeopardise their life's immunity. On the other hand, knowing that they are placed in front of a decision that deprives them of their free will, we could argue that their personal responsibility may be engaged only if they are actively supporting the unjust policies beyond what is constitutionally expected of them, thereby encouraging a continuation of the situation thanks to the transcendental aura they may have on their people and policymakers. One example in this regard could be King Umberto I, who ruled Italy when the country was a constitutional monarchy, which means that the Parliament exercised genuine political power. He was nonetheless killed in 1900 by an anarchist who was motivated by his desire to avenge the people killed in Milan during the May 1898 massacre that saw a debated number of protesters shot by soldiers with rifle-fire and artillery commanded by General Fiorenzo Bava Beccaris. As the decision to send troops was made by the Italian government and not by the king himself, we can say that the latter did not play any direct role in the bloody events that followed and, accordingly, did not engage his personal responsibility in the matter. However, the fact that King Umberto sent a telegram to congratulate Bava Beccaris for his actions and awarded him the Savoy Military Order actually changed his responsibility in the matter as his support showed that if he would have had the responsibility, he would have himself ordered the troops to open fire on the population.

Similarly, those upholding unjust policies, namely members of the military and police officers, also engage their responsibility in their country's unjust policies. This idea derives from the fact that these individuals' duty to obey is not absolute, as they are bound not to obey what are generally labelled as 'manifestly unlawful orders', which would imply refusing to obey orders that are contrary to international conventions, such as killing civilians and individuals deemed to be non-combatants. This element is a non-negotiable obligation on the part of individuals, such as soldiers or police officers, who cannot evade personal responsibility for their participation in unlawful actions they were ordered to commit. In this regard, the plea that they were under the unquestionable obligation to follow all commands from their superiors—even the most inhumane—is a non-receivable and legal dead end. In this sense, disobedience on the part of these people is a necessary way of ensuring that violence will be used in a humanitarian manner. Therefore, the real moral goal that the military (and other state-sponsored individuals who enjoy a monopoly of legitimate violence) ought to pursue is to protect the nation against domestic and foreign threats within the limits of the moral conventions of what is considered a just war. One of these conventions is defending one's state while simultaneously not harming civilians and the unarmed. For General Douglas MacArthur, respecting this rule was 'the very essence and reason' of his mandate as a member of the armed forces (Walzer, 2006, p. 317). Thus, soldiers' obligation to obey orders is valid insofar as they are legal. When this is not the case, disobeying them is a more stringent positional obligation on their part than their obedience duty. Consequently, soldiers who would nonetheless choose to participate in the implementation of oppressive policies that would be obvious violations of human rights would be engaging in their personal responsibility. As such, when the resort to violence is deemed to have met the aforementioned threshold, these individuals qualify as legitimate targets.

Finally, another category of individuals who would be affected by the loss of immunity would also include those who uphold a state's unjust and inhumane policy, who are not on the front line directly harming individuals like soldiers or members of the police forces, but rather in the shadows of the public administration. This category of individuals would include people like Adolf Eichmann or Reinhard Heydrich (because of his central role in the 'Final Solution to the Jewish question', his assassination in 1942 by a team of Czech and Slovak soldiers was therefore morally justified),[42] but also other low-level enforcers of policies acting in the civil service (Miller 2009, pp. 68–75).

The difficulty in distinguishing between those who are fully aware that their actions and decisions are instrumental in perpetrating inhumane crimes and thousands of civil servants who are unaware that their work contributes to the

---

42 In other words, the loss of one's immunity and becoming a legitimate target would be justified against people who are involved either as direct perpetrators in the violations of fundamental human rights or statesmen who imposes them. For Seumas Miller, the list of people affected by this criterion would be: '(...) politicians, or other non-military leaders, who are responsible for the rights violations, or the enforcement thereof, in the sense that in the context of a chain of command they were the relevant authority that directed that the human rights violations be carried out, or that they be enforced. Such civilians would also include persons who, while not necessarily part of any formal chain of command, nevertheless, were responsible for the rights violations (or the enforcement thereof) in that they planned them, and saw to it that other persons performed the rights violations (or the enforcement thereof)' (2009, p. 69). He also adds: 'Thus we can make the following claim about collective moral responsibility: if agents are collectively—naturally or institutionally—responsible for the realization of an outcome, and if the outcome is morally significant, then—other things being equal—the agents are collectively morally responsible for that outcome, and can reasonably attract moral praise or blame, and (possibly) punishment or reward for bringing about the outcome' (pp. 72–73).

enslavement of people, or do not think that their employment serves this purpose. For instance, we might wonder how an employee working in the state's water or aqueduct department might have the slightest clue that his work contributes directly or indirectly to these crimes, while an individual working in banks and who is now suddenly receiving from other state officials gold deposits in the form of eyeglasses or teeth could hardly claim the same lack of knowledge. The key here is probably to rely upon two conceptions of ignorance, namely 'vincible ignorance' and 'invincible ignorance'. The former notion refers to individuals who, despite being unaware of a wrongdoing, are nonetheless in a position to acquire information at their disposal that would allow them to realise the state of the wrongdoings. Further, the latter refers to individuals who are placed in a situation that would never allow them to make the same conclusions. Consequently, individuals who are not in a position to know about these unjust policies and are not in a position to stop them cannot be held morally responsible and retain their innocence and right not to be harmed in retaliation (Caron, 2019f). However, establishing that distinction might be easier in theory than in reality and the risk of attempting against the lives of individuals who are in a state of invincible ignorance is high. Consequently, this forces us to consider the theoretical aspect of the question considering the possible empirical repercussions of justifying a loss of life immunity of some civil servants and, thus, may lead us to the conclusion that attributing personal responsibility is an unreliable task that should not be used.

It is needless to add that once the aforementioned conditions have been met, even though guerrilla groups may be justified to resort to lethal actions against people who have engaged their personal responsibility in inhumane crimes, the morality of their attacks still depends on an important factor, namely that they must remain as discriminate as possible. However, when this is not the case, an attack against a legitimate target may nonetheless be considered immoral. Again, as previously stated, this has been a major ethical concern for guerrilla groups that have made their best to either cancel attacks at the last minute when it became obvious in their eyes that going forward with them would result in the likely death of innocent people or to severely judge those acting in their names who resorted to indiscriminate means of attack, such as the use of dynamite. For instance, killing a statesman involved in crimes against humanity may be morally justified, but fulfilling his assassination by planting a powerful bomb in an opera house where he enjoys the grand premiere of La Traviata alongside 500 other guests will contribute to transforming the rightful act into an act of unjustified terrorism.

Now that we have thoroughly discussed guerrilla warfare, it is time to investigate the most effective and moral ways of fighting terrorism. This is not a question to take lightly and calls for the necessary revision of the highly contested notion of pre-emption and also the necessity to rethink the most efficient sort of violence that ought to be used against these groups. This will be discussed in the next chapter.

Chapter 3
How to Combat Terrorism?

Now that a clearer assessment of what defines terrorism has been made, it is easier to understand the true nature of this type of political violence and its unique and immoral strategy: elements that help differentiate it from guerrilla—that is not exempt from its own ethical challenges. The following chapters will focus on the various ethical dilemmas associated with the fight against terror. This chapter will first explore the tension between two categorical imperatives: the state's obligation to protect the lives of its citizens and its obligation to limit the resort to war. In the last 20 years, this dilemma appears to be insurmountable, as illustrated by the cases of Afghanistan and Iraq. However, although I believe that this ethical dilemma is not insurmountable, it nonetheless requires the need to establish a fine balance between the former and latter obligations. This balance has not been properly established over the last 20 years of the war against terror because states have mistakenly believed that terrorism could only be fought effectively through war itself and not with other violent alternatives to war.

   Contrary to our beliefs, facing this type of threat comes with its own set of peculiarities and difficulties because of its indiscriminate violence that requires states targeted by terrorist organisations to proactively deter their attacks. In other words, this implies resorting to pre-emptive attacks. However, for reasons that will be discussed in this chapter, the conventional manner in which the notion of pre-emption has been developed and codified in the international norm does not apply for terrorism. Consequently, we are forced to rethink its criteria in a way that will allow states to effectively defend themselves and their citizens from these groups in a way that will not end up, and to justify unjustified large-scale attacks or wars against imaginary enemies, as was the case in 2003, when the US-led coalition invaded Iraq and overthrew Saddam Hussein.

Considering the way Western states have fought terrorism in the last two decades, it does not require a Ph.D. in political science to understand that large-scale attacks against states harbouring —or thought to be harbouring —terrorist organisations is an inefficient and immoral strategy. Indeed, military interventions in Afghanistan in 2001 and in Iraq two years later led to a terrible humanitarian crisis. In fact, it is estimated that 'During the war [in Iraq] and during the Islamic State militant group's occupation of as much as a third of the country in recent years, the number of deaths runs into the hundreds of thousands, including civilians killed as a result of violence and, more broadly, those who died be-

https://doi.org/10.1515/9783110757569-004

cause of the collapse of infrastructure and services in Iraq resulting from the on-going conflict' (Bump, 2018). Additionally, in October 2019 the Watson Institute estimated that a little more than 150,000 people have been killed in the Afgha-nistan war since 2001, 43,000 of whom were civilians (2020). In comparison, the 9/11 attacks cost the lives of 2,977 innocent civilians. These two cases are highly eloquent of how paradoxical the 'War on Terror' has been. Indeed, if these mili-tary interventions aimed to prevent the unjustified death of non-combatants, it is clear that they have merely transferred that risk (Shaw, 2005) to the Iraqi and Af-ghan civilians, as if 'our' lives were more valuable than 'their' lives: a premise no reasonable human being would dare defending. From this perspective, it is not difficult to understand why the fight against terrorism has been labelled by some as being terroristic as well.

Moreover, full-scale wars against terrorist threats have resulted in a lack of political stability and an incapacity to eradicate the menaces that led to their be-ginning. In the case of Afghanistan, US forces' withdrawal from the country in August 2021 has led those to return to power who once provided safe haven to Al Qaeda members in the years preceding 9/11 in a way that has prevented the United States from saving face by implementing what Henry Kissinger had once labelled a 'decent interval' (Caron, 2015). Furthermore, the toppling of Ash-raf Ghani's regime in only a few weeks also led to a terrible humanitarian crisis caused primarily by Western states who withheld the country's assets abroad. In-deed, to prevent the Taliban from establishing a stable government, the country was cut off from its foreign currency reserves and a significant part of its foreign aid that previously covered approximately 75% of the country's expenditures, es-pecially its health care system. Due to these sanctions, millions of Afghans are now struggling to survive and face starvation, and many healthcare facilities have been forced to close (Maizland, 2022).

In some cases, these interventions have been directly linked to the emer-gence of new threats, as was the case with the Islamic State following the 2003 invasion of Iraq. As we say in French, these interventions have led the US and its allies to undress Saint Peter to dress Saint Paul. Ultimately, nothing has really changed, and it is hard to claim victory when the eradication of the initial threat has led to the creation of another one, equally—and sometimes more—dangerous than the former. Thus, if these are the inherent disproportion-ate consequences of waging war against terrorism, there would be serious grounds to argue that this manner of dealing with such groups is morally ques-tionable, and that we must consider alternatives to full-scale wars. However, what could these alternatives be?

Because of its unforeseen consequences and potential dramatic impact on innocent people, war always ought to be the last resort. Consequently, non-violent alternatives to war (NVATW)—also referred to as 'soft war measures' (Gross, 2015; Gross & Meisels, 2017)—are integral parts of the vast arrays of measures that should be considered or employed against a foe to—as famously said by von Clausewitz—compel him to do our will. These include non-violent resistance, public naming and shaming, economic sanctions, arm embargoes, military assistance, and even non-kinetic/non-lethal cyberattacks.

Many historical examples have demonstrated the effectiveness of nonviolent resistance. For instance, Gandhi's movement that managed to liberate India from British colonial rule by relying solely on non-cooperation with the authorities, boycotting British products, or organising mass protests. Thus making the British presence in the country unprofitable and by generating guilt on the part of the occupying forces who are witnessing and sometimes collaborating to the suffering of those who are resisting passively[43], but also to crystallise the public opinion abroad at the sight of this suffering to generate international disgrace and pressure. In the same vein, public naming and shaming can also be effective in forcing a state to change a policy without having to undertake violent means of intervention. Indeed, states and their leaders are wary of being criticised by their counterparts which may impact their country's reputation and global influence. As this strategy can inform the global community about abuses and unjust policies, it can also contribute to labelling their perpetrators as pariahs which can then enable domestic activism and its support from abroad. Although we tend to focus on how a country's policy can be altered primarily through the prism of military or economic sanctions, we should not neglect how harming a country's international reputation may also lead to an expected change (Risse, 2000, pp. 29 – 30). This is especially true for countries whose global prestige and influence do not depend on their military power but rather on their renown for past deeds or policies that are thought to make other countries envious (Caron, 2012, 2022c). In this regard, we can mention the case of the South African apartheid regime and, more specifically, Canada's leadership

---

43 What Gandhi referred to as *satyagraha*, that is 'the sight of suffering on the part of multitudes of people will melt the heart of the aggressor and induce him to desist from his course of violence' (Tinker, 1971, p. 776). For example, as it was reported in 1930 by Negley Farson, an American correspondent for the Chicago Daily News, who witnessed the beating of a Sikh resister by police forces who were ordered to break up a non-violent protest with batons: 'No other Sikh had tried to shield him, but now, shouting their defiance, they wiped away the blood streaming from his mouth. Hysterical Indians rushed to him, bearing cakes of ice to rub the contusions over his eyes. The Sikh gave a smile and stood for more. And then the police threw up their hands. 'You can't go on hitting a blighter when he stands up to you like that' (Tinker, 1971, p. 778).

against Pretoria's policy of racial discrimination by publicly shaming South Africa in multilateral forums and in the country itself, thanks to its embassy to sustain global interest and to pressure the Afrikaner minority to end apartheid (Manulak, 2020).

Economic sanctions are another type of NVATW that can be used to compel an entity to alter its current policies by freezing its banks' assets, excluding it from services that allow worldwide financial transactions (as was the case following the 2022 invasion of Ukraine when Russia was excluded from the SWIFT system), or by imposing embargoes on the imports of certain products. James Pattison argued that economic sanctions are by far the most obvious and popular alternatives to military intervention, and their use has increased dramatically since the end of the Cold War, reaching over 300 between 1990 and 1995 (Pattison, 2018, p. 39). Arm embargoes can also be entertained to prevent the enemy from having the capacity to pursue aggressive policies and defend itself against potential military intervention against its territory. Providing military assistance to a country facing unjust aggression may also be perceived as NVATW in the sense that arming a victim may prevent the conflict from escalating into a regional or global crisis. In this regard, the Ukrainian case is a good example. By providing weapons to this country under attack, Western states could interfere with Russia's plans without having to wage war against Moscow, thereby limiting the scale of violence. Lastly, non-kinetic and non-lethal cyber-attacks can also be considered effective tools. For instance, cyber heists can count as measures short of war as they may contribute to hampering the capacities of an entity to strike an enemy by taking control of their financial assets (Caron, 2022d)[44].

However, none of these NVATW are considered panacea or magical solutions that will prevent states from resorting to violence. They all have flaws in terms of efficiency. Public naming and shaming will only be efficient if the entity targeted by this NVATW is sensitive to losing its international reputation. The impact of arm embargoes can be minimised when they are not upheld by all other state actors, when a state has the capacity to produce its own weapons, or when it can bypass these sanctions by importing them thanks to porous borders. Economic sanctions can also prove ineffective against states that have at their disposal their own sets of economic leverage, as is the case with Russia following its invasion of Ukraine, who can still export its oil and gas in elsewhere in the world, such as China, India or Pakistan. This can also be the case when they

---

[44] Thus far, the USD 81 million cyber heist of the Bangladesh central bank's account at the Federal Reserve Bank of New York by the Lazarus group in 2016 is the most famous.

are not upheld by the entirety of the international community or when the targeted country has a genuine capacity to survive thanks to an autarkic economic strategy. Furthermore, NVATW can emerge as highly immoral, as it can result in the indirect death of individuals, as is the case with the sanctions imposed against the Taliban following their return to power in 2021.

In our case, to the question of whether NVATW can be efficient at preventing terrorist attacks, I believe that the answer ought to be a careful yes. Like Michael Walzer wrote about these measures in the preface of the fourth edition of his seminal book, *Just and Unjust Wars* (2006), the NVATW that he has labelled as 'measures short of war' have proved themselves highly efficient at preventing Saddam Hussein from acquiring and developing any weapons of mass destruction (WMD) which he might have used either directly, or by supplying them to terrorist organisations (as well as preventing him from harming the civilian population in the northern and southern parts of the country, such as the Kurds and the Shiite Muslims). They were so efficient that they made the 2003 invasion of the country by the US and its allies unnecessary. As he writes:

> The harsh containment system imposed on Iraq after the first Gulf War was an experiment in responding differently [to a threat]. Containment had three elements: the first was an embargo intended to prevent the importation of arms (which also affected supplies of food and medicine though it should have been possible to design a "smarter" set of sanctions). The second element was an inspection system organized by the UN to block the domestic development of weapons of mass destruction. The third element was the establishment of "no-fly" zones in the northern and southern parts of the country so that Iraq's air power could not be used against its own people. The containment system was, as we now know, highly effective. At least, it was effective in one sense: it prevented both weapons development and mass murder and therefore made the war of 2003 unnecessary (2006, pp. xiii–xiv).

The ability to prevent aggression or mass murder without resorting to war also has a highly valuable moral advantage. Indeed, we must acknowledge that despite our best intentions and genuine attempts to respect the moral rules of warfare, full-scale conflicts always have tragic consequences for civilians, as has been the case in Afghanistan, Iraq, and more recently, Libya. In addition to the previously mentioned unforeseen and uncontrollable effects of full-scale wars, large-scale violence will always lead to the violation of the moral rules of warfare, more specifically, the principle of discrimination between combatants and non-combatants. This can be an outcome of various factors. Due to stress, fatigue, or a desire for vengeance, soldiers may end up targeting civilians. In an emergency, soldiers may confuse civilian buildings with legitimate military targets. Despite their sophistication, bombs and missiles can always malfunction and land in an unexpected environment. Although such risks may be minimal, they grow exponentially when the number increases to thousands. Therefore, we need to entertain the possibility that these unfortunate consequences may be prevented if we were to allow the use of measures that may effectively prevent terrorist organisations from attacking states in a way that would also prevent these sad consequences of war. In fact, we might even say that measures short of war are morally preferable to acts of war and must consequently be used whenever they are feasible.

Therefore, undoubtedly NVATW could be very effective against states harbouring or collaborating with terrorist organisations. However, it is also necessary to realise that the success of these NVATW is highly dependent on the fact that they have been designed to apply against state actors. Thus, there are reasons to question their effectiveness when it comes to stateless terrorist organisations. If economic sanctions can contribute to weakening the national economy in a way that forces a state to change its policy, this is obviously not an option against a stateless terrorist organisation whose functioning does not depend on the control of an economic market. If states' policies can be sensitive to public shaming and diplomatic sanctions, the same is not true for terrorist organisations, which have decided to wage an indiscriminate war against their enemies. Indeed, they do not fear that such actions may lead to a backlash against them, which is contrary to groups that have chosen to resort to guerrilla warfare because their strategy depends on the support of the population. If states can be affected by sport boycotts (Nixon, 1992), this cannot be the case with terrorist organisations, which could not care less about not being able to participate in the FIFA World Cup or the Olympics. Furthermore, if arms embargoes can hinder a state's capacity to arm its population or threaten international security, they have, on the contrary, very little effect on terrorist organisations that, similarly to organised crime, count on the black market to acquire weapons. If non-violent resistance can prove successful against an actor who is sensitive to its reputation (Holmes, 1989), it does not apply to certain actors who have no moral compass and who are immune from being shamed as they are unconcerned about what others think of their actions. Consequently, it makes it impossible to generate any leverage against them in a way that will force them to alter their course of actions and will remain unaffected by anything that is not emanating from their religious beliefs. In contrast, these measures will, in all likelihood, confirm the meaning and value of their actions. Therefore, non-violent options, namely non-cooperation with the enemy, are seen as tactically effective against a moral enemy, but not against one whose desire to realise the utopia he believes in takes precedence over any other strategic or moral considerations. The identity of one's enemy ought to play a fundamental role in our assessment of non-violent options, as philosopher Jan Narveson reminds us in his assessment of Nazis' lack of empathy and cruelty, quoted in the preceding chapter.

In case of terrorist organisations, this strategy can also prove inefficient against groups animated by an uncompromising opposition between good and evil or an apocalyptic worldview that supersedes any other strategic or moral considerations. In this case, if there are reasons to believe that the variety of measures short of war are not effective against terrorist groups, then states have the right to resort to violence against them. However, this conclusion brings us back to the numerous problems associated with war. If this is the only alternative at the states' disposal to fight terrorism, are they not doomed to act in a similar fashion as the groups they are fighting, hereby acting immorally as their enemies and often in pure loss if their resort to violence is not able to eliminate the terrorist threat? However, if they do not resort to violence against these groups, they are letting their civilians be seating ducks and not fulfilling their moral obligations towards them. After all, the duty to protect citizens is one of the most basic obligations of a state. Indeed, according to our modern tradition, governments are instituted to ensure the protection of their citizens, as argued by Thomas Hobbes, John Locke, Montesquieu, and Jean-Jacques Rousseau[45]. In other words, states have a contractual obligation to provide their citizens an environment that is better than any they could have in a state of nature. This obligation can take various forms. As argued by the European Court of Human Rights, 'This involves a primary duty on the State to secure the right to life by putting in place effective criminal-law provisions to deter the commission of offences against the person, backed up by law-enforcement machinery for the prevention, suppression and punishment of breaches of such provisions' (Kilic v. Turkey, 2000, p. 16). From this perspective, a state that refuses to act against a credible terrorist threat would be like a police officer waiting for a criminal to kill his hostage before taking forceful measures against the offender. I think most people would see this lack of proactivity as a form of negligence on the part of a state agent, which is detrimental to the political association's duty to protect those in danger[46].

---

45 Following this philosophical tradition, the US Supreme Court has adopted this perspective by saying that: 'the people (...) erected their Constitutions, or forms of government (...) to protect their persons from violence' (Calder v. Bull, 3 U.S. 386, 388 (1798)) and that 'the obligation of the government to protect life, liberty and property against the conduct of the indifferent, the careless and the evil-minded may be regarded as laying at the very foundation of the social compact' (City of Chicago v. Sturges, 222, U.S. 313, 322 (1911)).

46 Allen Buchanan and Robert Keohane share the same opinion. They wrote: 'Adherence to the [current legalist approach] is too risky, given the widespread capacity and occasional willing-

Consequently, states that are threatened by terrorist organisations seem to be caught in an ethical dilemma: they can either decide to protect their citizens by resorting to violence against terrorists. However, considering recent experiences in Afghanistan and Iraq, this will most likely come at the expense of thousands of innocent lives abroad. Moreover, they can abstain from taking such measures, which might expose them to an attack that could end up killing hundreds, if not thousands, of innocent people. Nonetheless, I would suggest that this ethical dilemma appears to be unsurpassable because we think of violent actions as inherently akin to war. This is a mistake and if we can think of NVATW, we should also think about 'violent alternatives to war (VATW)' as a limited form of violence that can respect both previously discussed categorical moral imperatives.

However, these VATW must be used in a preventative manner before the perpetration of an actual terrorist attack. What we must admit is that when struck at the heart of one's nation by fearless kamikazes who do not hesitate to use any weapon at their disposal to kill as many people as possible, those targeted by these attacks will obviously ask for revenge with all the possible means and military strength at their state's disposal. Unfortunately, after such attacks, it is not the time to call for moderation or for a proportionate reaction against the enemy. People want victory at all costs and they expect their statesmen to show extreme determination. This was clearly the case after 9/11 in the United States. Waiting to have suffered an attack from a terrorist organisation —that can be devastating if they employ WMD—before claiming to have a right of self-defence is therefore a bad and immoral strategy for reasons that have already been evoked. Consequently, this is another reason why initiating offensive actions to prevent attacks in the first place is the best course of action that states ought to consider. From this perspective, the only possible justification for the disposal of state entities is their right to pre-emptively attack those who threaten them and their citizens. However, the way this right has been understood since its codification in the 19th century is also very state-centric and, therefore, hardly applies to non-state entities like terrorist organisations which has led to a situation where the line between a pre-emptive attack and a preventive attack (which is illegal under international law and considered to be an act of war) has become blurred.

Following WWII, the UN Charter made a clear and conscious effort to limit the rightful use of force to exceptional circumstances. The main one was the right

---

ness of states and nonstate actors to deploy weapons of mass destruction covertly and suddenly against civilian population' (2004, p. 3).

to self-defence when sovereignty has been violated by another state[47], which allows states to defend themselves against aggression and also allows third parties to defend a state whose sovereignty has been violated[48]. Considering this restricted view on allowed violence, 'no other kind of warfare is allowed by international law unless explicitly authorised and endorsed—before-hand—by the United Nations Security Council (UNSC)' (Orend, 2013, p. 34). However, from a geopolitical and moral perspective, there are fundamental reasons to believe that such reactive measures should be avoided against terrorists. Indeed, when attacked by these groups, the appeal for revenge may take over, as was the case after 9/11, triggering a full-blown reaction resulting in a war that will not only destabilise the entire region, but also engender a previously-discussed situation where control over the events will be lost and where the uncertainties of war will unfortunately deliver their unwanted fruits. Moreover, as argued by Alex Bellamy, waiting to see one's citizens killed by terrorists before claiming to have the right to react is not only imprudent but also highly immoral and contrary to states' obligations to protect their people's natural rights, the most important being the right to life. Therefore, states ought to take a more proactive stance against terrorist threats. Unfortunately, the way in which this can be justified is state-oriented and cannot be applied to the menace posed by terrorism.

If the violation of another state's sovereignty is considered a *casus belli*, customary international law also allows states to proactively resort to violence when they face an immediate or certain threat of aggression. Such a situation is known as a pre-emptive war and finds its roots and principles in the *Caroline* incident of 1837, which involved the sinking of an American steamer operating on the Niag-

---

47 While Article 2(4) of the UN Charter states that 'All members shall refrain in their international relations from the threat or use of force against the territorial integrity or political independence of any state, or in any other manner inconsistent with the Purposes of the United Nations', Article 51 nonetheless allows states to resort to violence to defend themselves. It states: 'Nothing in the present Charter shall impair the inherent right of individual or collective self-defense if an armed attack occurs against a Member of the United Nations, until the Security Council has taken measures necessary to maintain international peace and security. Measures taken by Members in the exercise of this right of self-defense shall be immediately reported to the Security Council and shall not in any way affect the authority and responsibility of the Security Council under the present Charter to take at any time such action as it deems necessary in order to maintain or restore international peace and security'.

48 As was the case against Iraq in 1990 – 1991 when an international coalition repulsed Saddam Hussein's forces out of Kuwait after the small state had been annexed following a few hours of battle.

ara River by British forces[49]. However, because firing the first shot can easily be perceived as an act of aggression, it is necessary for states to claim that such an action was triggered by a threat to their sovereignty, to prove that it was actually the case. In this regard, *Caroline* jurisprudence states that the threat in question must have been 'instant, overwhelming, leaving no choice of means and no moment for deliberation'. Walzer has reformulated this idea with three criteria, namely that the enemy displays 'a manifest intent to injure' and 'a degree of active preparation that [makes] that intent a positive danger' in such a way that 'waiting, or doing anything other than fighting, greatly [magnifies] the risk [to the state being targeted by this threat]' (2006, p. 81). For him, the Six-Day War of 1967 constituted a good example of a pre-emptive attack that met these criteria. Indeed, three weeks before Israel struck the first blow, the UN announced that its Emergency Force, which had served as a buffer between Israel and Egypt in the Sinai since the end of the Suez Canal Crisis, was to be withdrawn. The Egyptian armed forces immediately reoccupied this territory, while the Egyptian government closed the Gulf of Aqaba and the Strait of Tiran to the Israeli boats. Concomitantly, the Egyptian armed forces were put on maximum alert and mobilised, while military alliances were signed with Jordan, Syria, and Iraq. Finally, Gamal Nasser, the Egyptian President, declared on 29th May that in the eventuality of a war against Israel, his 'goal would be nothing less than [its] destruction' (Walzer, 2006 p. 83). Faced with these threats, Israel attacked its enemies on 5th June as it became clear to its government that it was only a matter of days before the country would be under attack.

Justifying this form of anticipated violence is seen by its proponents as a matter of justice against a would-be aggressor who is already guilty because of his intent to commit illegal action that might result—as is unfortunately the case with any war—in the killing of innocent people. As suggested by J. Warren Smith:

> Lesser evils may be necessary to avoid greater evil. There are two ways in which the greater evil may be identified. First, there is a utilitarian standard. The death of the one brigand is preferable to the deaths of many innocent travellers that will occur if the brigand is not stopped. Second, there is the standard of justice by which each man should receive his due. The killing of the brigand is an evil but it is preferable to allowing the death of an innocent man. The death of the traveller is a greater evil precisely because the traveller is innocent and so does not deserve death. The death of the brigand is a lesser evil because he is

---

49 The criteria for a legitimate pre-emptive attack are themselves inspired by the work of Hugo Grotius (1583–1645), for whom anticipatory self-defence ought to be allowed when there is a present danger and a threatening behaviour that is imminent in a point of time.

already guilty by virtue of his evil intention. The greater evil to be avoided is allowing injustice to be perpetrated (2007, p. 146).

According to this conceptualisation, a pre-emptive action ought to be understood
strictly as an act of self-defence. In such cases, it is an anticipated form of self-
protection, as contrary to opposing someone or an entity that has already struck
the first blow. It is intended to be used against a person or entity that poses an
actual threat. The whole question is to determine when a threat moves from 'potential' to 'real'. After all, if we are to harm individuals who have still not hurt us,
morality imposes on us the obligation to prove that our action is justified because our enemy's upcoming attack is certain. As summarised by Suzanne Uni-
acke, the notion of 'imminence', deemed to have been present in the aforementioned case of the Six-Day War, plays a pivotal role in the assessment of a threat.
She writes:

> (...) Striking before one is struck can reasonably be regarded as self-defense only if it ap-
> proximates closely to an act of retaliation, a return of harm. This is why the imminence
> of the attack being preempted is significant to the representation of restricted instances
> of preemption as self-defense. (...) Outside of these conditions, the use of preemptive (pre-
> ventive) force against a (merely) possible or potential threat is not an act of self-defense. A
> person acting in self-defense aims to prevent the infliction or imposition of a harm or a
> wrong; he does so by resisting or repelling an actual, or under certain conditions an immi-
> nent threat. In contrast, preventive force aims to prevent a possible or potential threat from
> becoming an actual threat, by means of disabling a possible or potential threat from be-
> come an actual threat, by means of disabling a possible or potential aggressor (2007, p. 80).

Allowing states to defend themselves against such threats bears many similarities to domestic laws. Indeed, while people are not allowed to unjustly attack
their co-citizens, they are allowed to defend themselves after they have been attacked or when they feel threatened by a genuine menace which means that
would normally constitute a crime. In the case of a pre-emptive attack, people
can defend themselves only if the threat is imminent and credible. In this
case, simple verbal threats not accompanied by a clear intent and means to fulfil
them would not justify resorting to defensive actions.
    It is easy to understand why resorting to forces outside of these peculiar sit-
uations can be problematic. Indeed, if force ought to be tolerated in the domestic
sphere simply based on someone's fear of eventually being attacked, it may lead
to a generalisation of unjustified violence against individuals who may not be
motivated by any form of animosity. In the realm of inter-state violence, deadly
large-scale wars may be waged against political entities under the same excuse,
which is problematic, as threats are an essential component of the dynamics of

the international community. Simply put, because of its destabilising effects, war should only be an option when all others have failed or are no longer available. This is why David J. Garren (2019), similarly to Hugo Grotius, is right to highlight that mere suspicion and fear do not constitute solid grounds to justify resorting to anticipatory self-defence actions that may prove deadly. To limit violence as much as possible, self-defence needs to remain a highly restricted option that must be circumscribed by the presence of ongoing harm against oneself, the certainty that harm will occur, or the imminence of harm that can only be repelled with violence[50]. Accordingly, the right to anticipatory self-defence can only exist when a threat against us is 'coming or likely to happen very soon', 'ready to take place' or 'hanging threateningly over one's head' (Lubell, 2015, p. 702).

However, because of the reality of the world order following WWII, this understanding of legitimate violence can work when dealing with conflicts between states. However, since the end of the Cold War, with an increasing number of civil wars and those being fought by non-state actors, as in the case of terrorism, this has not necessarily been the case[51]. Thus, the assumptions upon which just war theory was constructed in the post-1945 world are not in tune with certain features of contemporary conflicts. First, clearly, contrary to states, the terrorist groups previously discussed are not risk-averse entities against whom the traditional forms of deterrence will work. If, in the past, WMD were an effective way to defend one's sovereignty through fear of mutually assured destruction, this is no longer the case against these terrorist groups. More precisely, because of their stateless nature and the fact that their members seek martyrdom through their actions, governments targeted by terrorist groups are in dire need of finding new ways to avoid their attacks (Bush, 1 June 2002). However, this comes with another problem, as pre-emptive logic is of little use against terrorist groups

---

50 He gives the following example: 'If you knew that in a week's time you were going to be stricken with an irreversible form of paralysis that would leave you unable to move or speak, and knew that once stricken your enemy was going to take advantage of the opportunity to kill you, would it be permissible to kill him first, in advance of the paralysis, or would you have to wait and take your chances? (...) If you knew to an absolute certainty that you were going to be paralyzed, that it was irreversible, that your adversary was going to kill you and that nothing short of killing him would stop him from doing so, I think that a compelling argument might be made that your right of self-defense would permit such an anticipatory measure. The obligation not to use lethal force first is, after all, a defeasible one and it might well be defeated here, the abundance of certainty (with respect to options and outcomes) compensating for the lack of imminence (with respect to threat)' (Garren, 2019, p. 204).

51 C.A.J. Coady wrote: 'the last quarter of the twentieth century and the beginning of the twenty-first century have seen a dramatic decline in warfare understood as direct state-to-state conflict' (2008, p. 4).

that are no longer willing to discriminate between combatants and non-combatants. Indeed, contrary to state actors, it is challenging to effectively prevent a terrorist threat from occurring through the logic of pre-emptive self-defence (Buchanan & Keohane, 2004, p. 3), which makes the war against terror unique. Unless some concrete information about an upcoming terrorist attack becomes available, the previously mentioned imminence criterion that cannot be assessed with these groups is lacking here; because of their *modus operandi*, these elusive enemies are able to covertly attack and kill thousands of civilians without any precursory signs. Contrary to state actors planning to violate another state's sovereignty, terrorist groups do not display the mass mobilisation of troops and military equipment alongside their enemy's borders. Because of the asymmetrical nature of their fight against great powers, their success rather relies on the element of surprise, which Noam Lubell summarised as follows:

> The challenge posed in the context of imminence is that, in effect, we are faced with a threat, for which we cannot positively identify how soon it might happen, where it will originate from, where it will strike, or even who precisely will be behind the attack. (...) the threat of terrorism plays on the fear of the unknown, and raises the question of engaging in self-defense to prevent a possible future attack without knowledge of what it might be. As such, it challenges not so much the interpretation of imminence, but the effect calls into question the very existence of the imminence requirement. (...) the idea of acting to prevent a vague and non-specific threat cannot, therefore, be covered within the concept of imminence (2015, p. 707).

Indeed, adhering to the notion of imminence against this type of threat is a recipe for disaster. Owing to terrorist groups' surprise attacks and their potentially apocalyptic use of WMD, waiting for their threats to become immediate is suicidal (Beres, 1991; Glennon, 2002). Thus Dominik Svarc argued:

> The particularly grave threats which could materialize in attack without a reasonable degree of warning and time for defense may be regarded imminent even when the attack is not menacingly near. (...) Applying the narrow temporal standard of imminence in such contemporary reality might deprive a State from an opportunity to effectively repel the attack and protect its population from unimaginable harm. It would go counter to the object and purpose of the right of self-defense which provides States with a self-help mechanism to protect them from an attack when peaceful alternatives would prove inadequate and the multilateral response too tardy (2006, p. 184).

In this sense, it is difficult to criticise former President Bush for his assessment of the terrorist threat during his 7th February 2003 State of the Union Address in which he said the following: 'Some have said we must not act until the threat is imminent. Since when have terrorists and tyrants announced their intentions, politely putting us on notice before they strike? If this threat is permitted to fully and suddenly emerge, all actions, all words and all recriminations would come too late'. The problem deriving from this dilemma is that not rethinking how the principle of pre-emption ought to apply against terrorist organisations would simply result in merging it with the notion of 'preventive war/attack' that ought to remain illegal.

Reassessing the pre-emptive attack logic is highly controversial and comes with serious concerns as, as said by Deen Chatterjee, the '(...) US war on terror [against Iraq is] an example of what could go wrong with [a more permissive logic of political violence]' (2013, p. 2). The most important of these concerns is the adoption of an overly generous view of what constitutes an imminent threat, which would lead to a legitimisation of wars against entities that are not really a menace, ultimately leading to further destabilisation of the world order by setting off 'a cascading series of "preventive" attacks or interventions' (Bethke Elshtain, 2013, p. 23). However, because of the terrible consequences of terrorist attacks and the inherent difficulties in foreseeing them, there is a need to act before these groups strike, which creates an incredible dilemma. As per legal theorist George Fletcher, there is a legitimate reason why we ought to avoid an unlawful strategy that prematurely legitimises the resort to force and, contrarily, to come up with an approach that makes retaliation the sole option after a terrorist attack (1998, p. 133).

Many solutions have been suggested in the wake of the 2003 Iraq intervention. For instance, many authors pointed out that the possible collaboration between this rogue state in possession—as it was thought at the time—of WMD and a terrorist organisation was clearly a recipe for disaster. As Stephen Strehle puts it:

> [Iraq's] relation to terrorism is a matter of grave concern. It provides a special channel to deliver and promote his wicked designs. Bin Laden has called it a "religious duty" for his minions to obtain and use WMD against the infidels, but he knows that his terrorist network needs help. It is only in the movies that Dr No is able to create the facilities to manufacture and deliver WMD. In the real world of terrorism, the capacity to make and utilize these weapons requires the help of a government. Aum Shinrikyo, a Japanese cult, tried to kill thousands of commuters with a potent nerve agent but managed to kill only a dozen after spending somewhere around thirty million dollars. The loss of these lives was tragic but much less than expected and displayed the complexity of operations using these agents. The cult was not able to produce the chemical (sarin) in sufficient purity and resorted to using a most primitive delivery system—carrying it on a train and piercing bags of it with tips of umbrellas. A government working with a terrorist organization would produce a more lethal combination (2004, pp. 77–78).

In the event of such a collaboration between a state and a terrorist organisation, the obvious fear is that once the former provides the latter with a WMD, it will already be too late to react as this weapon will vanish until it is used in a surprise attack against thousands of innocent civilians. Thus, there is a need to act before the terrorist organisation can manage to get its hands on such weapons. For Strehle, no one should be expected to be threatened by such a menace against their lives and 'the mere possibility' that a terrorist organisation would be able to have WMD at its disposal justifies its 'immediate elimination' (2004, p. 79). Jean Bethke Elshtain followed a similar logic in her justification of the intervention in Iraq (even after it took place[52]). For her, because there is a strong possibility that criminal regimes will engage in wrongful actions, the case for intervention becomes stronger. In a nutshell, this is the logic used by the White House at the time President Bush ordered the invasion of Iraq. Unfortunately, such a criterion is highly problematic, as it is still based on fear that is not or may never be founded in the future. This opens up the risk of interpreting too broadly what constitutes a threat, leading to interventions against unfounded threats and, consequently, the unjustified direct or indirect suffering and deaths of innocent people (Schweller, 1992, pp. 236–237). The lack of evidence that Saddam Hussein possessed WMD and collaborated with Al Qaeda and the terrible consequences of this invasion should make us wary about considering this criterion a plausible one. In this regard, 'fear' as a criterion should be abandoned as possible grounds to justify resorting to violence against an enemy[53].

In fact, we may question the desire to eliminate fear in the field of politics. Furthermore, it is perfectly understandable for people and states to want to live in a peaceful world untampered with the fear of seeing one's security being challenged. However, simultaneously, we cannot ignore the fact that it is not only an unachievable political dream, as it is in the nature of other states to always seek to maximise their power and influence over other entities, but that it is also not desirable for societies. Indeed, as argued centuries ago by Augustine, a small dose of fear can be highly beneficial to societies as it allows for the development of well-needed social virtues, namely vigilance and a willingness to protect and

---

52 She wrote in 2006 that the intervention was justified (2006, p. 110).

53 Ancient and modern authors believed that fear has often been the leading cause of wrongs in the past. As Xenophon once wrote in *Anabasis*: 'For I know that there have been cases before now—some of them the result of slander, others of mere suspicion—where men who have become fearful of one another and wished to strike before they were struck, have done irreparable harm to people who were neither intending nor, for that matter, desiring to do anything of the sort to them'. Grotius also shared a similar assessment of how we should be wary of fear as a criterion to justify the resort to violence (*De Jure Belli ac Pacis*, 2.1.5.1)..

defend institutions that allow people to be free and enjoy basic human rights[54]. In contrast, when individuals are no longer fearful, there is a risk that they will lower their guard and will not be able to foresee a real threat from arising. For Augustine, it is precisely this lack of vigilance caused by their lack of fear (which led to *apatheia*) on the part of Roman citizens that favoured the conflicts between Marius and Sulla or Pompey and Caesar (*The City of God*, I.30). In our liberal democratic era, following the well-known arguments of Benjamin Constant and Alexis de Tocqueville, it is the fear that statesmen might abuse their power and deprive us of our freedom that forces us to remain vigilant to all their comings and goings. Whether we like it or not, there is undeniable value in fear.

However, what I believe to be the most promising path is to focus on a notion that is as important as imminence when assessing a possible threat against us, that is, how *credible* it is. Indeed, not all threats are the same, and if some are frivolous, others ought for their part to be taken seriously. This distinction is made possible by assessing its reasonableness in light of the peculiarities of the threat itself. Let me proceed by using a few examples that will hopefully allow the reader to get a better view of the criteria that can be used to make that assessment. For instance, let us imagine, on the one hand, a drunk customer in a pub, who is barely able to stand on his feet, openly threatens the bartender to kill everyone in the bar if he is not served one more drink and, on the other hand, three individuals wearing masks and who are holding sawed shotguns and a sports bag full of grenades threatening to kill everyone is the bartender is not handing them over the money from the cash register and the safe hidden in the backroom. What would obviously make the assessment of the reasonableness of these two threats entirely different is their respective credibility in the eyes of the beholder, which would also affect people's reactions. If, in the second scenario, customers are allowed to resort to all possible actions, including the use of deadly force, against the three men, a similar reaction against the stumbling customer would not be deemed commensurate and proportionate with the nature of his threat. Therefore, having and displaying the means to achieve one's ambitions is a fundamental variable to consider.

---

[54] As a Christian thinker, Augustine primarily saw in fear a capacity to elevate men so they could reach the City of God. As J. Warren Smith wrote in this regard: 'the struggle against fear is part of God's training humanity in the way of true justice. Rather than escaping fear by eliminating its temporal causes, Augustine argues that we must live with our fear so as to place our hope upon the kingdom to come. There is a sense that living with fear is living with the reality of death and the threat of our judgment by God. Living with such knowledge cultivates humility' (2007, pp. 149–150).

As has been said, only the credibility of the threat in the eyes of the beholder should be considered. For instance, let us imagine that a man walking his dog in a park is suddenly threatened by someone holding a handgun, who is asking him to choose between his wallet and his life. However, this turns out to be an empty threat as the weapon is either not loaded or loaded with blank rounds. At the exact same time, a police officer on duty is witnessing these events and clearly hears the perpetrator threatening the innocent walker. There is no doubt that he would be justified in using all possible means, including lethal ones, against a man holding a weapon. In this case, the threat is sufficient to justify retaliation, because of its credibility. In no means, the police officer must wait until the perpetrator actually pulls the trigger before intervening. If he were to use his service pistol to neutralise the menace, and it was later discovered that the perpetrator was not actually in a position to harm anyone, it would not make the police officer's decision any less legitimate. Credible threats to people's lives have always justified resorting to potential lethal countermeasures against their perpetrators, irrespective of whether they are willing to transform their threats into reality. In such a case, the appreciation of the threat is assessed solely from the perspective of the person on the receiving end[55].

From this perspective, we can better judge the characteristics of a credible terrorist threat. It is, of course, possible to adopt a view of what defines such a threat as the one developed by David Luban, who believes that a threat is credible when its propensity for future armed attacks is clearly based upon characteristics such as 'militarism, an ideology favouring violence, a track record of violence to back it up, and a build-up in capacity to pose a genuine threat' (2004, pp. 230–231). However, the first two criteria are, in my view, too broad as using them to justify violence against people would be similar to trying to justify deadly retaliation against the drunk customer in the previous example. A simple warlike rhetoric would not be sufficient to justify retaliatory actions against members of an organisation formulating it. For this threat to be considered credible, it would need to be backed up by evidence that the group in question has the capacity to fulfil its menace or is actively trying to acquire the means to reach that end. This logic bears in my mind many similarities with the way Randall R. Dipert has defended the resort to some forms of anticipatory actions in the absence of a threat actually being imminent. For him, when a threat is substantial and waiting for a potential attacker to strike first poses a serious risk, there

---

55 This is also known in criminal law as the 'reasonable person standard', namely that a person is entitled to resort to defensive force insofar as her decision to act as such resulted from a belief any other reasonable person would have had.

are grounds to justify anticipatory actions. He gives the example of a belligerent neighbour who has previously attacked you and your family without reason and has sworn openly to do it again. Thanks to the mailman who informed you that the man has delivered hand grenades, a machine gun, and an RPG, you know that his previously formulated threat can now be fulfilled. Although you do not know precisely the day and time of his attack, Dipert argues that these facts would certainly constitute legitimate grounds for a preventive attack (2006, pp. 37–38). It is certainly difficult to disagree with him. However, through this example, Dipert unconsciously adds another criterion to his list, that is, the fact that your neighbour now possesses the means to fulfil his deadly ambitions. Until it is actually the case, his threat—although very worrying—is nonetheless not credible, as he lacks the means to realise it. In my view, this element is required if we are to justify anticipatory attacks that currently fall outside the current logic of pre-emptive war. Relying solely on Dipert's first three criteria is not sufficient, as they would allow states to attack any threatening entity, irrespective of its capacity to actually do so. In hindsight, this view could lead to a generalisation of political violence and, therefore, contribute to the merging of preventive attacks with pre-emptive ones.

While this criterion can be troubling for some who might consider it to be too generous, it must nonetheless be said that it is in fact the cornerstone of the R2P principle and of humanitarian interventions that preceded its codification in international law back in 2005. In fact, this idea was used quite successfully in 1991 against Iraq, following the liberation of Kuwait. Soon after the Desert Storm Operation, a civil war ignited in the northern and southern parts of Iraq after the Shiite Muslims and Kurds launched military operations against the Iraqi forces, which remained loyal to Saddam Hussein. This was mainly the result of President Bush's explicit encouragement of the Iraqi people to overthrow their dictator,[56] which led them to believe that they would be supported by the US forces if they chose to fight. However, as it turned out, President Bush was only offering moral support[57] and soon after attacking Iraqi forces and taking

---

56 In his remarks in front of the American Academy for the Advancement of Science on 15th February 1991, President Bush said the following: 'But there is another way for the bloodshed to stop, and that is for the Iraqi military and the Iraqi people to take matters into their own hands to force Saddam Hussein the dictator to step aside and to comply with the UN and then rejoin the family of peace-loving nations' (quoted in Malanczuk, 1991, p. 117).

57 The insurgents were most probably victims of the *raison d'état*. As Peter Malanczuk wrote: '(...) in view of American interests in the region as a whole, it did not mean support for a division of Iraq in the wake of the Shiite insurrection in the south and a corresponding Kurdish uprising in the north. On the contrary, the territorial integrity of defeated Iraq needed to be secured in

control over garrisons in early March 1991, the momentum quickly shifted. This was made possible despite the fact that Saddam Hussein's military forces had suffered a crushing defeat because the Iraqi dictator had been able to prevent his elite Republican Guard units and a large number of his tanks from being captured or destroyed by the coalition forces by agreeing to a ceasefire about 100 hours after the beginning of the US-led offensive to liberate Kuwait. Equipped with helicopters, combat aircraft, and heavy tanks, Iraqi forces took control of their lost territories. In the north, the counter-offensive led to a massive refugee crisis when about one million Kurds fled into the mountains, fearing their lives. Their reaction was triggered by the Anfal genocide, to which people had been victims for nearly 30 years. In its earliest stage, the policy, which was also known as 'Arabisation', was mainly oriented at displacing Kurdish families from the region to other areas of Iraq where they were monitored by the Iraqi military and given minimal food and water, which led many to their deaths. In return, with the clear aim of altering the demography of the northern part of the country, poor Arabs were encouraged to move to abandoned houses of these families. This policy was also associated with the mass murders of men of military age and detention in the harsh conditions of Kurdish women and children. Over this period, nearly one million Kurds were estimated to have died. However, the most remembered event of this genocide certainly remains the Halabja chemical attacks in March 1988, when the Iraqi regime resorted to the indiscriminate mass gassing of an entire town through the use of sarin, VX, and mustard gas that killed at least 5,000 people and injured approximately 7,000 civilians. With little food as well as inadequate shelter and clothing for the harsh conditions of the cold mountains, it was estimated that between 1,000 and 1,500 refugees died daily. Faced with the distress of Kurds, the West decided to act. On 7th April, the US began Operation Provide Comfort by airlifting food and medicines to the refugees, and the following day, John Major, the British Prime Minister, asked for the creation of a safe zone in the area that would provide security to the Kurdish people, and President Bush finally agreed to a few days later. This latter action, which led to the creation of a no-fly zone above the 36th parallel that remained effective until the 2003 invasion, effectively cut off Saddam Hussein's regime from the northern part of the country and protected

---

order to preserve Iraq's function as a balance, primarily against Iran. Although the Islamic Republic did not say so officially, it was clear that only Iran had an interest in a successful Shiite revolution in the south of Iraq. The establishment of an independent Kurdistan in the north of Iraq, on the other hand, not only would have raised the issue of control over the important oil resources in the area, but also would have posed a threat to the security of neighbouring States, in particular Turkey' (1991, pp. 117–118).

the Kurds from further exactions. In the 12 years that followed its creation (as well as the no-fly zone in southern Iraq created in August 1992 to prevent human rights violations against Shiite Muslims), many limited interventions occurred either when the Iraqi Air Forces attempted to breach the exclusion zone or when the Iraqi armed forces showed aggressive intent. For instance, in September 1996, 44 cruise missiles were launched against Iraqi air defence targets as retaliation after Saddam Hussein launched an offensive in Iraqi Kurdistan. In September 1992, an American F-16 shot down an Iraqi Mig-25 caught flying inside the southern no-fly zone. Alongside these restrictions, following the adoption of Resolution 687 by the UN Security Council, Iraq also had to submit to a series of sanctions that prevented Saddam Hussein from using, developing, constructing, or acquiring chemical, bacteriological, or nuclear weapons. Iraq is also limited in its capacity to import and export goods. The objectives of these sanctions were to prevent the mass murder of Iraqi civilians as well as another invasion of Kuwait, and to eliminate Iraq's capacity to use WMD.

As argued by former Marine Corp Commander General James Jones, this proved to be 'one of the greatest American military operations of the 20th century' (2017). Through its soft approach, the US-led coalition was not only able to provide effective humanitarian aid to a vulnerable population, but also allowed the Kurds to return home and live peacefully until the 2003 invasion. Moreover, the effectiveness of this second set of sanctions cannot be denied. Despite the claims made by the Bush administration prior to the 2003 invasion, Saddam Hussein's regime did not produce WMD following its defeat against coalition forces in 1991 after the liberation of Kuwait. Walzer thus argued that the effectiveness of this containment system made the war of 2003 unnecessary (2006, pp. xiii–xiv).

While this is undeniably true, we must admit that the imposition of no-fly zones is illegal under international law. Indeed, preventing the Iraqi air forces from operating on a significant part of its national territory and being the victims of surgical strikes were clear breaches of Article 2, Paragraph 4 of the UN Charter. This was clearly stated in April 1991 by the UN Secretary-General, who perceived the intervention as a serious, unjustifiable, and unfounded attack on the sovereignty and territorial integrity of Iraq (Malanczuk, 1991, p. 124). On the contrary, and similarly to what Walzer has said, many people would argue that there is little room to pretend that this intervention was not justified from a moral perspective. I believe that most people would come to this conclusion because of Saddam Hussein's proven lack of consideration for human rights, with the Kurdish genocide being the most explicit example. From this perspective, resorting to the aforementioned forceful measures that limited Iraq from enjoying full political sovereignty could be seen as a precursor to what became known in the 21st century as the R2P principle. This means that the success of such humanitarian interventions has more to do with the logic of preventive than pre-emptive wars, since the notion of imminence cannot always be assessed in the same way as when we are facing a conventional conflict between two states, as in 1967 with Israel and its Arab neighbours. To prevent civilians from being massacred, it might be necessary to assess imminence in a manner that places a higher value on conjectures and intentions than on the clear evidence of an upcoming attack.

The case of Iraq in 1991 is a good example. Superficially, it is easy to justify the restrictive actions imposed on Iraq based on the need to prevent civilians from genocide. In fact, this rhetoric was used by political leaders such as Masoud Barzani, leader of the Kurdish Democratic Party, who called on the international community to help stop the genocide against the Kurds, and Germany's Foreign Minister, Hans-Dietrich Genscher, who described on 5th April 1991 the actions of the Iraqi military as akin to a genocide (Malanczuk, 1991, p. 119). This opinion is shared by analysts such as Samantha Power (2002, p. 241), who has seen in Operation Provide Comfort an unprecedented intervention that marked the beginning of a new post-Cold War era in terms of genocide prevention. However, at that time, there was no empirical evidence of an ongoing violation of human rights against the Kurds or of any plans to pursue actions similar to those in Halabja a few years before. Of course, as mentioned before, many of them were dying daily in the mountains of northern Iraq, but this was the result of the civil war itself and not the direct exactions of Saddam Hussein's men. If the interventions by the US-led coalition were based on a humanitarian perspective and for genocide prevention, they were not the result of a clear and imminent threat that the Iraqi government had resumed or was about to resume its mass murder policy against the Kurds, despite the rhetoric used at that time by those who were advocating for an intervention. Accordingly, what is striking about the 1991 sanctions is their preventive nature as a possible counterattack against Kuwait, or the coalition forces with the use of chemical or nuclear weapons was not imminent at all. The same can be said regarding genocidal actions against the Kurds. The limitations on Iraq's sovereignty were mostly the result of the fear that Saddam Hussein might have resumed his previous deeds in the aftermath of his defeat. At no point was the international community certain that this would happen, or that the killing of members of this minority group was imminent. The 2011 crisis in Libya also demonstrated how unpredictable human rights violations could occur. As said by Ruben Reike, 'It is interesting to note that at the time that the first protests erupted, Libya was not considered to be at risk of mass atrocities or violent conflict by any of the various risk assessment mechanisms' and 'Despite Gaddafi's notorious record on human rights, the country was widely seen as relatively stable' (2012, p. 126).

Considering this, why did the decisions to intervene in Iraq and Libya seem appropriate from a moral perspective? I argue that the statements made by the Iraqi and Libyan regimes, as well as their capacity to fulfil their threats, made these fears credible and justified acting against them. I believe that this point is the cornerstone element of a revised view of what constitutes an imminent threat considering the new nature of contemporary political violence. We cannot ignore the fact that in a speech made on 16th March, Saddam Hussein said that Iraqi armed forces would crush the Kurds with all possible means, including the use of chemical weapons. The fact that Iraq had previously shown its utter lack of respect for the Kurds and its willingness to use this sort of weaponry against them made that threat even more credible. Moreover, despite its quick defeat against coalition forces, the Iraqi military still had at its disposal the necessary equipment to resume its genocidal campaign against the Kurds, outweighing them with heavy tanks, helicopters, and planes. If we were to follow the logic of the pre-emptive attack, we would have had to wait for Iraq to manifest a degree of active preparation for the Kurdish population before acting against the regime. However, because these attacks can be planned covertly and performed very quickly, standing under the conventional logic of pre-emptive war would have meant waiting for the Iraqi military to resume the gassing of its Kurdish minority before taking action against Saddam Hussein. If the price to pay waits for the start of the actual murder campaign before acting, the R2P principle simply loses its purpose and brings us back to situations such as those in the 1990s.

In a context where imminence cannot be assessed and civilian lives are at stake, the intentions of an actor with the means to fulfil its ambitions are sufficient criteria for the justification of actions aimed at preventing the menace from ever being carried out[58]. In theory, applying these criteria would have allowed the international community to prevent the genocide of Rwanda. If there were no signs that allowed the peacekeepers on the ground to foresee the genocide hours or days before it actually started on 7th April 1994 their commanding officers nonetheless had evidence that it was going to happen at some point. Indeed, as reported by General Roméo Dallaire, who was leading at the time the UN Assistance Mission for Rwanda—in his book *I Shook the Devil's Hand* and in many of his interviews—it was obvious many months before the beginning of this humanitarian tragedy that a genocide was being prepared by some

---

58 As Emer de Vattel wrote in the 18th century, 'power alone does not threaten an injury: it must be accompanied by the will' (Book 3, Chapter 44).

Hutus. On several occasions, he sounded an alarm. On 20th January 1994 an informant warned the Canadian general that radical members of the Hutu government were planning to eliminate Tutsi. More specifically, he was informed about the existence of four separate weapons caches in Kigali filled with machetes, AK47s, and grenades, revelations that were confirmed during the second week of February, when another informant revealed similar information[59]. Even though the prospect of a genocide in Rwanda never met the conventional criteria of imminence that might have justified the resort to pre-emptive measures, it was clear months before it started that the radical Hutus had the means to fulfil their intentions of eliminating whom they called the 'cockroaches'. However, no one listened to General Dallaire, which led to one of the most dramatic humanitarian tragedies of the 20th century, despite the fact that the threat was credible by all means.

In this sense, the mass murder of civilians shares similarities with the potential terrorist attacks. Indeed, both can be triggered with little or no warnings, and once it is the case, it is already too late to act. Accordingly, to save civilians from being massacred, actions that fall outside the scope of how the category of pre-emptive attack is understood.

However, what are the types of alternatives to war that ought to be used pre-emptively against terrorist threats? Since they are violent and expected to fall short of being considered acts of war because of their scale and effects, they refer to actions such as the targeted killing of members of terrorist organisations and the destruction of specific infrastructures that are used to produce weapons that might ultimately be employed by them. It is important to note that, because of their lethal and kinetic nature, these actions ought to be as discriminate and proportional as possible. In this regard, many studies have focused on drones that have been privileged in the last 20 years, as the weapons of choice for targeted killings were thought to be immoral tools because of their propensity to kill a significant number of innocent people (Chamayou, 2015). More precisely, a

---

59 General Dallaire sent cables to Kofi Annan, then head of the UN Department of Peacekeeping Operations, about this information and that his informant had been ordered to register all Tutsi in Kigali, which he suspected was a way to facilitate the future killings (...). He was also horrified to hear the propaganda of Hutu extremists echoed in the media, notably the newspaper *Kangura* and the *Radio Télévision Libre des Milles Collines*, calling explicitly for the elimination of the Tutsi (Thompson, 2007, pp. 1–12). Therefore, General Dallaire repeatedly asked his superiors for more freedom regarding the UN mandate that did not allow him to disarm the militias. He also sought to block the Hutu radio transmissions and asked for the sending of more UN peacekeepers. However, all his demands were refused and his worst fears became a reality in April 1994.

2009 report from the Brookings Institute argued that for every terrorist killed at the time by a drone strike in Pakistan, an average of 10 civilians were also killed, thereby making the civilian-to-combatant ratio an astonishing 10:1 (Byman, 2009). However, as I have already argued elsewhere (Caron, 2021), it is important to not confuse the inherent morality of a weapon with the way it is being used. If antipersonnel landmines and chemical weapons ought to fall in the former category either because of their inability to distinguish between combatants and non-combatants or because of the inhumane sufferings they are causing, drones do not have these flaws. A drone strike is no different from an artillery shell falling in an enemy's position or a sniper killing the foe he has in his sight. Indeed, all these weapons bring death, but not by causing inhumane suffering. Furthermore, what needs to be said about drones' inability to discriminate between combatants and civilians is not due to their peculiar design or functioning like mines but rather by the way they have been used. In this regard, the high number of killings of innocent people by American drones resulted from what is called 'signature strikes', namely attacks against unknown individuals whose behaviours are considered suspicious according to certain patterns-of-life analysis. For instance, individuals seen digging a hole and hiding something on the side of a road or individuals gathered in a group and shooting in the air with their weapons will likely be targeted because their behaviours will certainly be interpreted as typical of terrorists planting improvised explosive devices or a terrorist training camp, while these individuals can, in reality, be farmers of people participating in a traditional wedding (Chamayou, 2015, p. 50). On the other hand, when drone strikes are used against specific individuals who are known for their involvement in terrorist groups that are posing a credible threat (what is called a 'personal strike) and with proper rules of engagement (that is, the release of weapons will not be allowed by the commanding officer when the individual is surrounded by innocent people), drones can be highly effective means of eliminating in a way respectful of the moral rules of warfare a terrorist menace. In other words, when judging a weapon's inherent morality, it is a mistake to focus our attention solely on how it is being used.

Obviously, these lethal and kinetic forms of violence are more loaded from a moral standpoint than their non-violent counterparts since their aim goes beyond the mere pressure to compel our enemies to alter their course of actions, but rather implies depriving them of their most basic natural right. Thus, these violent actions ought to be allowed only after NVATW have proven themselves or are thought to be ineffective in countering the terrorist threat. In my view, these are the most important principles for respect.

1. Lethal and kinetic actions can only be justified against enemies who are, based on reliable, authentic, and confirmed information from multiple

sources independent from one another, posing a credible threat to civilians. More specifically, they have at their disposal the means to effectively transform their menace into reality or are actively trying to achieve this goal.

2. These violent and destructive measures are only permitted when NVATW are thought or have proved themselves to be ineffective at eliminating terrorist threats.

3. The goal of resorting to lethal and destructive measures must solely be to eliminate the identified threat, and must end as soon as the menace has been eliminated.

4. Lastly, the choice of appropriate violent and destructive measures must be made on the basis of achieving the objective in a proportionate manner that will limit the potential harm to innocent civilians as much as possible.

Consequently, because of their violent and destructive nature, these measures should therefore be labelled 'violent alternatives to war' or 'VATW'. But, why are they to be considered as 'alternatives to war' since they are implying the use of violence? Indeed, even though Article 2(4) of the UN Charter clearly states that states should refrain from resorting to the threat or use of force against the territorial integrity or independence of another member of the international community, it did not ban actions that take a non-forcible form, such as economic sanctions. Even though NVATW are aimed at infringing on a state's capacity or willingness to pursue a specific course of actions, they are not considered as violations of article 2(4) of the Charter and can therefore be rightfully considered as 'alternatives to war' (Neff, 2005, p. 318). However, apart from the use of force as a means of self-defence to repel an attack on one's sovereignty, against an imminent attack about to be launched or the UN Security Council authorised resort to armed force[60], the use of violent means of action against another state is generally considered akin to an act of war. In this regard, it is therefore worth questioning whether the use of lethal and kinetic violence against terrorist organisations or states harbouring them can really be qualified as 'alternatives to war'.

This is a complex question that can be assessed from empirical and judicial perspectives. First, many states have established their own interpretations of resorts to violence that do not in their mind meet the threshold for an act of war. For instance, even though lawyers and scholars do not largely support this view, Israel and the United States have adopted the idea that 'defensive reprisals' are legitimate VATW when they are used in the aftermath of a terrorist attack as a way to deter future incidents. 'Rescue missions' that may imply the use of mili-

---

60 Which was the case in Korea in 1950, in 1991 for the liberation of Kuwait and in 1994 in Haiti.

tary force on foreign territory, as it was the case in 1976 when Israeli special forces intervened to liberate hostages who had been taken by terrorists who highjacked an Air France airliner in Uganda, are also considered by some states as legitimate violent actions that do not amount to acts of war. Second, even though various court decisions have for the most part used a very narrow and traditional view of what ought to constitute a legitimate use of force without being considered as an act of war, the International Court of Justice has famously stated in the *Nicaragua v. United States* case of 1986 that not all resorts to force can be qualified as an armed attack with the effect of triggering a collective right of self-defence (International court of Justice, 1986, par. 211 & 249), particularly when the violence does not reach a certain threshold of gravity.

What appears to be the red line when violence ought to be considered an act of war is the scale of the attack. Consequently, contrary to the general assumption, it is a mistake to conclude that all resorts to force and violence are akin to acts of war (Gartzke, 2013, p. 54). There are many disagreements regarding what constitutes this threshold. For instance, David J. Singer and Mel Small argued that violence degenerates into war when there are 'at least 1000 battle deaths' (1972). For his part, Brian Orend has written that war is defined by the resort to an intentional and heavy quantum of force (or its imminent use) that is preceded by a significant mobilisation of military personnel and the deployment of military equipment on a large scale (2013, p. 2–3). According to this definition, the 2003 invasion of Iraq or the 2022 invasion of Ukraine were clearly acts of war. Of course, it is possible to quarrel about the nature of the intensity of force required before reaching the threshold that allows for the differentiation between an act of war and an action that falls short of being considered as such. According to Jessica Wolfendale, this intensity ought to be measured by the level of disruption caused by a conflict with those living in the arena of conflict (combatants and civilians), including the impact on their physical safety, access to basic goods such as food, water, warmth, and shelter, and the functioning of basic civilian infrastructure. In other words, a conflict meets the criterion of intensity when it becomes so disruptive that civilians' ability to meet their basic needs is seriously threatened, and the local authorities are unable to effectively control the conflict and protect civilians and civilian infrastructure from harm (Wolfendale, 2017, p. 21). The VATW are far from meeting this threshold.

Therefore, it is problematic to establish, as is the case with Michael Gross and Tamar Meisels, a dichotomy between NVATW defined as 'soft war' measures[61] and those involving violence as being constitutive of 'hard war' mea-

---

61 For them, the notion of soft war refers to non-kinetic actions that fall short of armed attacks,

sures. With such a distinction, actions that are not considered 'soft' are *de facto* akin to 'the stuff old-fashioned wars are made of' (2017, p. 1). As VATW have nothing to do with what 'old-fashioned wars' were about and because there are reasons to argue that they are not acts of war, I find it rather unfair to present them as equivalent to 'mass killing fields [and] wholesale deaths in battle (...)' (2017, p. 1) as if there were only one form of political violence. On the contrary, because they imply killing and maiming (2017, p. 3), they do not fit within the 'soft war' category. This is why NVATW and VATW should simply be called measures short of war, as they bear several similarities with the sorts of actions that were understood as such in the 19th century and during the first half of the 20th century. These measures, accepted by the international community as not being akin to acts of war, were mainly seen as measures of law enforcement and limited in terms of scope and aims. Political intervention in the affairs of other states fits this definition. Stephen C. Neff reminds us in his seminal book on the evolution of conflicts (see Chapter 6, 2005) that the European powers that prevailed against Napoleon in 1815 were primarily motivated to prevent any kind of future conflict on the continent and gave themselves—France joined them in 1818 after it was safely back under the rule of Louis XVIII—the responsibility of maintaining the status quo and the balance of power. Thus, Austria intervened in Naples and Sardinia in the 1820s to restore peace and stability after domestic events led to the destabilisation of these kingdoms. It follows the logic that France intervened in Northern Spain and restored the authority of King Ferdinand VII after insurgents had taken control of that part of the country, or why a naval blockade was imposed against Greece in 1886 after it had launched an offensive against Bulgaria. Similar actions were also undertaken for the sake of what would later be known as 'humanitarian intervention' to prevent the massacre of a civilian population. This was the case in 1860, when France sent troops to Lebanon, when communal violence posed a threat to the lives of civilians.

Reprisals were also thought to be measures short of war that did not amount to acts of war; rather, they were seen as forceful means to pursue a just cause. The 1907 Hague Convention on the Opening of Hostilities made it clear that reprisals were not akin to acts of war. These actions were seen as justified only after a state that had been the victim of an injustice expressed grievances against the state responsible and asked for reparatory measures. If the solution was unsatisfactory, the former state was allowed to employ forceful actions that were

---

such as 'bytes, boycotts, propaganda, non-violent resistance, and even kidnapping' rather than 'bullets and bombs' (207, p. xv). In this sense, their understanding of such actions is very close to NVATW.

deemed proportionate to the gravity of the offence; actions that had to cease immediately after a satisfactory solution had been obtained. A good example of a reprisal was the French seizure of the Turkish Port of Mytilene in 1901. Neff wrote the following:

> The purpose was to induce Turkey to provide satisfaction to France for a number of alleged infractions of international law to the detriment of French nationals, which France carefully identified in a diplomatic note. There was no violence or destruction. Moreover, the action was successful in inducing Turkey to reach a settlement of the dispute with France, after which France duly evacuated the captured area. It was observed, apparently without irony, that the incident was "a truly ideal reprisal", involving no loss of life, no infringement of the interests of the third parties and a wholly satisfactory outcome (for France, that is) (2005, p. 228).

Emergency actions employed by the state to defend itself from what it considered an imminent danger were also deemed measures short of war. This was the case in 1807 after the British destroyed part of the Danish fleet in the port of Copenhagen and took control of the rest, despite the fact that the two countries were not at war. The reason was simply to prevent Napoleon's troops, quickly approaching the Danish capital, from taking control of the fleet and using it against the royal navy. A more contemporary example is the destruction of the French fleet at Mers-el-Kébir in 1940, after Marshall Pétain signed an armistice with Germany. Churchill and the British Cabinet feared that the powerful and modern battleships stationed in the harbour would fall into German hands and then be used by Hitler in his openly stated intention to invade British Isles. Following an ultimatum that was left unanswered by the French, orders were given to British Admiral James Somerville to destroy the fleet. The attack, which was described by Churchill as 'the most hateful decision, the most unnatural and painful in which [he had] ever been concerned,' led to the death of more than a thousand French sailors.

The rescue of nationals in peril abroad, as well as punitive expeditions, were also considered measures short of war. The British government resorted to the former action in 1868 against Ethiopia after its emperor decided to hostage a consular official and a government envoy. After an ultimatum had been rejected by the Ethiopian Head of State, the British Army launched a successful military expedition that stopped after the hostages were freed. Punitive expeditions were also tolerated by individuals or groups who had committed wrongdoings against a foreign state. This was the case when the American military entered Mexico in 1916–1917 to capture Pancho Villa after he killed American citizens taken from a train in Northern Mexico and after he burned down a city in New Mexico, which also resulted in the death of 19 American citizens.

As argued by von Clausewitz, because of their aim, none of these measures were considered akin to acts of war, mainly because 'the hostile spirit of a true war' was lacking. On the contrary, they were perceived positively because measures short of war did not possess an *animus belligerendi* on the part of the state that used them. They were used not to promote mere selfish national interests but for noble intentions such as preventing instability, saving lives, self-defence, or punishing individuals who had committed crimes. Moreover, the limited impact of these measures and their low intensity allowed statesmen and lawmakers to distinguish themselves from acts of war. In many ways, NVATW and VATW share the same fundamental goal as that underlying the application of measures short of war in the 19th century and the early decades of the 20th century, namely, to prevent the outbreak of a full-scale war.

Of course, VATW ought to be employed by states following terrorist attacks rather than full-blown wars. Indeed, as the last 20 years have shown us, war is not only a disproportionate measure against these groups that comes with the previously evoked consequences, but also a hugely ineffective one. Contrary to a state that can be defeated and against whom peace can be achieved following an armistice or formal peace treaty, terrorism can only be prevented with the appropriate anticipatory measures that have been discussed or contained at best after these groups have already struck[62]. The large deployment of troops can do very little against an idea that will end up inspiring lone wolves or small cells all around the world and who will strike devastating and murderous blows at civilians who calmly enjoy an evening walk on a boardwalk or a drink on a terrace, or simply read a book on the subway on their way to work. This Sisyphean strategy is doomed to bring endless wars and destruction, as well as engendering a situation that will paradoxically lead to what states are supposed to prevent, that is, the death of tens of thousands of innocent civilians. This is why these sorts of VATW that are accepted forms of violence—even if they are still illegal according to international law—ought to be considered the right form of retaliation following a terrorist attack rather than war. However, this is a valuable strategy for this study. Indeed, because of the strong desire for revenge that can result from a terrorist attack, there are reasons to doubt that a sense of moderation will

---

62 This unique nature of the war against terrorism was rightly acknowledged by President Bush during his 20th September 2001 joint address to Congress in which he warned Americans that 'This war will not be like the war against Iraq a decade ago, with a decisive liberation of territory and a swift conclusion'. At that time, his appraisal of how terrorists had to be fought was appropriate as well. Instead of thinking of conventional means of warfare, he rather evoked '(...) a lengthy campaign, unlike any other we have ever seen [which] may include dramatic strikes, visible on TV, and covert operations, secret even in success'.

dominate in the aftermath of such an attack, a possibility that simply provides an additional argument in favour of resorting to VATW in a preventative way.

In conclusion, the apparent ethical dilemma resulting from being forced to choose between inaction and war is not an insurmountable problem if we are to admit the need to codify VATW as a valuable tool for the disposal of states to prevent terrorist groups from striking. When used properly, they can allow states to fulfil their duty to protect the lives of their civilians, as well as those of people who have the misfortune of living in regions where terrorist organisations are operating. However, this requires us to reconsider the principle of pre-emption. Not doing so comes with an obvious risk; as they do not have the capacity to protect their civilians against terrorism, states will be tempted to launch preventive wars, as was the case with Saddam Hussein and Iraq in 2003. In light of the current deficiencies, alternatives, such as the one defended thus far, need to be found. Not acting in this regard means that every resort to anticipatory VATW will simply contribute to eroding the value and relevance of international law in favour of subjective and questionable assessments of the terrorist menace that may well come with disproportionate and indiscriminatory measures. At the end of the day, as argued by Oscar Schachter, acting outside the law, even for legitimate reasons, runs the risk of losing the name of law and creating global cynicism (1984). This ought to be avoided at all costs, which is why I believe that anticipatory VATW as a response to contemporary terrorism must become an integral part of international law.

Chapter 4
The Status of Captured Terrorists

A second ethical dilemma, usually associated with combating terrorism, is the tension between the state's obligation to protect its citizens' lives and the obligation enshrined in the international norm not to harm an individual who has surrendered its combatant status. In other words, are states allowed to resort to methods akin to torture captured terrorists? Similarly to the dilemma discussed in the third chapter, I do not perceive this tension as being insurmountable when it is able to meet some very specific criteria.

As it is an unconventional form of violence, terrorism entails very specific challenges that cannot necessarily be met with the traditional tools of just war theory. The previous discussion about the necessity to go off the beaten track to figure out novel ways of fighting this threat more efficiently and in a more ethical manner through a revised version of pre-emption. This shows that it is sometimes possible to find what I believe is a morally acceptable amendment to the conventional rules of warfare that were not originally developed against this type of threat coming from non-state actors without resorting to unbalanced strategies that can turn up as both immoral and strategically problematic. When this is the case, the chief objective ought to be to limit as much harm as possible and to use it when it is truly a last-resort option. Other challenges typically associated with terrorism should also be met in the same way, namely how terrorists ought to be treated upon capture. Some have argued that they cannot be considered POW and that, accordingly, the Geneva Conventions should not apply to them. Although there are reasons that can justify a differentiated treatment for terrorists, they must nonetheless remain within the limits of what can be morally defendable, and the harm must be kept to an absolute minimum as well as a last resort option only when it is absolutely necessary for the sake of protecting civilians' lives. From this perspective, claiming a total departure from the moral rules of warfare simply on the basis that states are facing a situation that was not taken into consideration when the moral rules of warfare were established should never give *carte blanche* to statesmen and members of the military so that they can get their hands dirty without limitations. Revising a rule in light of unforeseen circumstances does not mean abandoning every ethical restraint, but rather finding a balance between the exceptionalism of the situation and the risks it entails with the ethical obligation to limit permissible harm. This is discussed in this chapter.

https://doi.org/10.1515/9783110757569-005

For people living in liberal societies, torture is, for the most part, a historical curiosity for tourists visiting old European castles and their inevitable torture rooms or of infamous buildings where the Gestapo and later the NKVD were performing their terrible deeds against opponents, such as Budapest's 'House of Terror'. This terrible treatment was also thought to be the sole domain of authoritarian and totalitarian states that are still famously known for not abiding by the United Nations Convention on Torture. However, for law-abiding democratic societies, the moral weight of human dignity is so strong that 'the legal prohibition of torture is widely understood as a peremptory rule, as derogation is considered impermissible' (Bellamy, 2006, p. 126). For this reason, when Italian authorities were invited to consider resorting to torture after its former Prime Minister Aldo Moro had been kidnapped by the Red Brigades, it was decided that 'Italy [could] survive the loss of Aldo Moro, but it [could not] survive the introduction of torture' (Dershowitz, 202, p. 134).

As a consequence of this belief, nobody thought prior to the 9/11 attacks that a liberal nation like the United States would choose to resort to this type of violence against members of Al Qaeda. Even though the government has repeatedly refused to acknowledge that it was practising torture, rather opting for the expression 'enhanced interrogation techniques', this semantic game was not able to hide the fact that waterboarding and depriving captures terrorists of sleep were clearly torture methods. Indeed, even though these methods can be considered 'more civilized' than the 'Judas Cradle', the 'Pear of Anguish', the 'Iron Chair', the 'Rat Torture' or the 'Head Crusher', they are nonetheless aiming at inflicting deliberate pain on vulnerable individuals who are totally at the mercy of their tormenters for the sole purpose of extracting information from them.

The case of torture is well known since Cesare Beccaria wrote about it in the 18th century. Calling this practice cruel and barbaric, Beccaria also emphasised the fact that torture implies assuming that an individual is not innocent despite the fact that he has not been found guilty by his peers. In this regard, he was referring to the Medieval practice (that extended all the way to the French Revolution) of the 'ordinary' and 'extraordinary questions' imposed on individuals suspected of a crime. In the former case, it consisted of a muscled interrogation with the purpose of extracting a confession, while the latter method was used to obtain a more thorough admission of guilt. To achieve this goal, numerous systems were invented, such as 'the boot' which consisted of wooden boards nailed together around the victim's leg with wedges hammered between them to create pressure until he either admitted of his guilt or until his bones were shattered. In the case of the ordinary question, four boards were used and eight when a more thorough interrogation was needed.

This basic assumption against torture as an immoral mean remains valid today and why it is thought to be 'the most profound violation possible of the dignity of a human being' (Sussman, 2005, p. 2). Indeed, individuals who may be victims of torture can be imposed a form of violence that is not external to their body but rather emanates directly from it. In other words, torture implies the betrayal of our own body against our autonomy and freedom that is not only momentaneous, but still vivid even after the torture has stopped (and we cannot do anything to stop that pain that will forever remain a part of ourselves). This is obviously the case with broken bones that will leave individuals unable to manage certain tasks or do certain movements for the rest of their lives, such as the late Senator and US Presidential nominee John McCain who after having been tortured by the North Vietnamese at the infamous 'Hanoi Hilton' after his capture, could no longer lift his arms above his shoulders. However, this is also the case with the psychological pain experienced by tormenters against their victims, which will have life-lasting effects. In this regard, we can consider the example given by David Sussman regarding inmates at Abu Ghraib prison:

> It is perhaps not accidental that many of the most common forms of torture involve somehow pitting the victim against himself, making him an active participant in his own abuse. In Abu Ghraib, captives were made to masturbate in front of jeering captors. Here the captive was forced into the position of having to put his most intimate desires, memories, and fantasies into the service of his torturers, in a desperate attempt to arouse himself for their amusement. The U.S. soldiers could beat and kill their prisoners, but only the prisoner himself could offer up his own erotic life to be used against himself in this way (2005, p. 22).

Therefore, we cannot count as torture other psychological techniques used by police forces throughout the liberal world that do not degrade the detainees of their dignity and do not result in long-lasting trauma, such as befriending the detainee in order to gain his trust or putting in his cell an undercover police officer whose task is to extract information through banal conversations once reciprocal trust has been established between them.

Another reason why torture is deemed problematic is that it is deemed ineffective at extracting valuable and reliable intelligence. Indeed, victims' only hope to stop the pain is to provide their captors with whichever information they wish to hear. This can also be an involuntary outcome of some torture techniques, such as sleep deprivation. Studies on insomnia and observations of intense military training have shown that a lack of sleep tends to halter in a significant way people's capacity to think clearly up to the point that individuals tend to forget their own name (O'Mara, 2015, pp. 148–168). This conclusion was also made by individuals who resorted to torture in Algeria and Vietnam, namely generals Paul Aussaresses and Jacques Massu during the former war and colonel Carl Bernard and major F. Andy Messing in the latter, who agreed that information obtained under duress was generally unreliable (MacMaster, 2004, p. 12).

In this regard, other non-coercive interrogation techniques have proven to be more efficient at extracting information, such as the ones used by Hanns Scharff during WWII, also known as the master interrogator of the Luftwaffe. Scharff became an expert in what is referred to as 'information elicitation', that is gathering information in a way that the source will remain completely unaware of the true intent of the interrogator, which was made possible by developing trust and befriending allied crewmen who had been shot down by sharing his coffee with them, taking them to the movies or for a walk. In other words, by being able to imagine himself in the prisoners' shoes, he chose to display an attitude towards them that was entirely devoid of hostility and which crewmen were not expecting from the Nazis (Granhag et al, 2016, p. 135). Once this true had been established, he was able to extract information by casually discussing what appeared to be trivial matters, not by asking direct questions (which would have been too obvious for the prisoners), but rather by stating information with the expectation that the sources would confirm its accuracy. This is how he learned that the white smoke left behind by American tracer bullets was a signal that the plane would soon run out of ammunition. This attitude was coupled with other important features, namely the interrogator's capacity to give the impression that he already knows the information given by the prisoner and to downplay any new information the latter might reveal as unimportant. In the first case, believing that the interrogator is already aware of specific information, the sources will not have the tendency to hold back secret details that may turn out to be new to the interrogator. More precisely, 'The 'illusion of knowing-it-all' leads the source, to some extent, to misperceive what information the interviewer holds; as a result, the source is more likely to unknowingly reveal new information' (Granhag, 2016, p. 139). In the second case, by not showing immediate curiosity and insistence on any new information revealed by the sources, the prisoner will not realise that he might have revealed valuable intelligence.

Another reason we ought to be wary of allowing torture is what appears to be the inevitable slippery slope that comes with it. As it has been argued by Christopher Tindale (1996), all countries that have allowed torture to be used in exceptional cases have all ended up normalising its practice and have extended it to 'ordinary' criminals and political opponents. The war in Algeria is a good example. If torture was used at the beginning only against individuals suspected of terrorism, it began in 1957 as a common practice used against all those who were arrested by the French authorities (Bellamy, 2006, p. 144; Pellissier, 1995; Branche, 2001). When this happens, such a situation runs the risk of leading to a decay of liberal values and a certain banalization of evil. It is from this perspective that Neil MacMaster wrote:

> Torture, widely referred to as '*la gangrène*', was seen as a form of cancer that inexorably led to the degeneration of the liberal democratic state, its institutions (particularly the army and the judiciary), its core values and fundamental respect for human rights and dignity. The centrality of torture to the debate on the Algerian war lay not in the grim horrors of the practice as taken in isolation, but rather in the extent to which it served as a symbol of a deeper corruption, both of the state and of the structures of military, administrative, and judicial power that had made it possible (p. 9).

These are the most common objections to the use of torture, and it is not my intention to thoroughly examine them in this chapter. My goal is to analyse whether the belief that torture may be an appropriate way of combating terrorism, which has emerged in numerous respectable political and legal circles in the Western world since the 9/11 attacks, can be defended.

Despite its numerous criticisms, many authors have argued that because of terrorism's inherent *modus operandi*, torture ought to remain tolerated in some exceptional circumstances against individuals suspected of being involved in this type of political violence. For them, the harm torture would generate would be outweighted by their ability to prevent much greater harm to innocent people. This is notably the case with Henry Shue, who, after having vilified those who advocated for the use of torture on a wide scale, nonetheless went on to argue that forms of enhanced interrogations may be justified in exceptional situations[63]. This is also the case with Bernard Gert who wrote that 'there are extreme cases in which all rational men would agree that, even if the evil is to be switched from one person to another, there is a point at which the amount of evil to be pre- vented by breaking the rule is so much greater than the amount of evil caused by breaking it, that one ought to break it' (1969, p. 623).

Treating captured terrorists differently than conventional POW is not an insignificant idea as it goes against the *jus in bello* rule that enemy combatants must be treated humanely at all times and protected against acts of violence that include torture in order to obtain information regarding the situation of their armed forces. What motivates this belief is that unlike conventional soldiers, the capture of terrorists does not necessarily transform them into non-threatening entities. To better understand this idea, it is important to remember

---

[63] He writes: 'it cannot be denied that there are imaginable cases in which the harm that could be prevented by a rare instance of pure interrogational torture would be so enormous as to outweigh the cruelty of the torture itself' (1978, p. 141).

how the killing of soldiers has been justified, and the notion of self-defense is central to this debate. It is believed that all combatants are considered to pose a potential threat to their foes once a war begins. The reason is that 'soldiers as a class are set apart from the world of peaceful activity; they are trained to fight, provided with weapons, and required to fight on command. No doubt, they do not always fight, nor do they war their personal enterprise. But it is the enterprise of their class (…)' (Walzer, 2006, p. 144). This explains the essence of the principle of discrimination, and why soldiers should not deliberately harm civilians. If combatants pose a potentially lethal threat to other combatants, this is simply not the case for individuals who are not soldiers. As summarised by Jeff McMahan,

> Those who retain their immunity to attack are therefore those who are not threatening. In the context of war, the innocent are those who do not contribute to the prosecution of the war—that is, non-combatants. The non-innocent are those who pose a threat to others—that is, combatants. They lose their immunity and are liable to attack (2006, p. 24).

The loss of immunity will, therefore, only affect soldiers, irrespective of the side they fight on, because they can potentially harm other combatants by joining their country's armed forces. Known as the 'symmetry thesis', this refers to the moral equality of combatants. In return, since non-combatants are by definition unarmed and do not pose a threat to anyone, killing them would not be a matter of self-defense but murder. This category includes civilians and members of the military whose duties make them harmless—like chaplains[64]—or who are prisoners of war, surrendering, or defenceless because of unconsciousness or wounds[65]. When soldiers are in combat on the battlefield, resorting to lethal violence is thought to meet the criterion of necessity, as shooting first at an individual who is armed and trained to obey at any time an order to kill you is the only way to prevent him from harming you. Indeed, it would be inconceivable, for example, for a sniper to scream at the enemy soldier he has in his sight that he should surrender or be shot. Not only would it allow this enemy combatant to escape from the threat and fight another day, but it would also allow his comrades to know where the sniper is hiding and take proper measures to take him out. In return, soldiers have the obligation to use proportionate actions when they are in such a situation as a way to prevent as much as possible

---

64 Protocol 1, 8th June 1977, Article 43.2 states that chaplains are non-combatants and that they do not have the right to participate directly in hostilities.
65 Provided that they are not showing any sign of hostility or trying to escape.

any collateral damage that may result in the harm of individuals who have not lost their immunity against harm.

This unique status of soldiers also opens the door to the targeting of those who have been labelled 'naked soldiers', that is, members of the military who are engaged in actions that are not battlefield activities and who do not pose a direct threat (Deakin, 2014, p. 321). Although Walzer admits that shooting an enemy combatant who is taking a bath in a river behind enemy lines might be psychologically troublesome for many individuals who could feel that because of his vulnerable condition the soldier in question is no longer an enemy but rather a 'normal man', he still believes that this person remains a legitimate target. For Walzer, the logic behind this conclusion lies in the fact that the naked soldier is not similar to an enemy combatant who has surrendered or is wounded and unable to continue fighting. In such cases, these soldiers regain their status as non-combatants and should, accordingly, be treated with humanity and respect. Not doing so would be a war crime. However, as von Clausewitz has argued, all soldiers, even the naked ones, have abandoned their status of 'normal men' by joining the ranks of the military and by submitting themselves to its martial virtue (von Clausewitz, 1976, p. 144). According to this logic, the naked soldier remains in a position to harm other soldiers in the future. It is in this sense that Stephen Deakin wrote that 'like a tank, artillery piece, or a military aeroplane, the naked soldier is a weapon of war. Destroying tanks, guns, and the like is a legitimate and desirable activity in war whether they are in use or not at the time, and the same is true of naked soldiers' (2014:329). Even if the naked soldier or unused military equipment does not pose imminent danger, they may nonetheless pose a credible threat because they may resort to or be used for lethal purposes against other individuals, which justifies their killing or destruction.

However, when a soldier is captured or surrenders, he immediately ceases to be a potentially lethal threat to his enemies, which is why it is no longer acceptable to try to harm him. When these situations occur, and unlike the case of a naked soldier, the captured or surrendered combatant becomes a non-threat on a permanent basis, as he will be held in a POW camp until the end of the conflict, and consequently regains his immunity from being harmed or killed. This is not thought to be the case with terrorists in certain situations that Shue and Gert are referring (known as 'ticking bomb scenarios') that are referring to the following circumstance: a man who has planted an explosive device in a highly (but unknown) crowded place is arrested. It is assumed that this bomb will go off within the next hour, and police forces have no way to prevent this from occurring. In such cases, the capture of a terrorist does not eliminate the threat, and, consequently, the category of *jus in bello* is not thought to apply to them and calls for captured terrorists to be subjected to another logic that we may call the *jus in custodia*. One of the many elements of the latter notion[66] is the resort to methods akin to torture. The first challenge in this regard is determining the circumstances under which the resort to this type of violence could be excused.

When we are facing the ticking bomb scenario, should we be allowed to do everything in our power to find the location of the bomb and disarm it (or at least evacuate the location) in order to save the lives of innocent people who are threatened by this terrorist? This is the opinion of Shue who '[sees] no way [of denying] the permissibility of torture in a case *just like this*' (1978, p. 141)[67] or of Walzer for whom being confronted with these sorts of dilemmas is unfortunately a key feature of governance and that those in charge may be required at times to 'get their hands dirty' (1973). Having to make such a decision appears to be a genuine case of an ethical dilemma, as respecting one categorical imperative will inevitably harm another. In this case, the tension is between refusing to torture a suspect that would result in the death of civilians (not respecting the obligation to prevent individuals from being harmed or killed) or harming a suspect to save the lives of innocent people (violating the physical integrity of a defenceless individual).

I would argue that privileging the former imperative over the latter is made easier by the fact that, similarly to the question discussed in the previous chapter, ethical tension is flawed by the fact that those who are the victims of the state's political violence are not thought to be innocent or to have regained their immunity against being harmed. Indeed, it is possible to argue (and this

---

66 Another important one is whether they should be sentenced to penal sanctions for their involvement in a terrorist organization. In the case of conventional POW, insofar as they have not been personally involved in violations of *jus in bello* obligations, being a soldier does not entail such consequences. Disciplinary sanctions of POW are however allowed, such as against prisoners who are making escape attempts. However, these sanctions should not entail corporal punishments or any treatment deemed to be cruel. Another important point is about the release of POW and of captured terrorists. If in the case of the former, article 75 of the 1929 Convention relative to the treatment of prisoners of war provides that the repatriation of POW shall begin as soon as possible after the conclusion of peace, the question is more chaotic since the wars against terror are apparently endless. This is especially the case with the global war on terrorism that officially started on 9/11 which is still on-going.

67 In the kidnapping case of Louis Gachelin (which I am discussing in this chapter), a US tribunal conceded for the first time in the early 1980s that a distinction must be made between violent conduct of police forces for extracting a confession to save lives and to obtain information through coercion in order to secure a confession (Leon v. State, 410 So. 2d 201 (Fla. Dist. Ct. App. 1982). The court of appeals approved the actions as necessary for 'a group of concerned officers acting in a reasonable manner to obtain information they needed in order to protect another individual from bodily harm or death'.

is my claim) that an individual who is actively planning a terrorist attack or who is in possession of information about an imminent threat to the life or well-being of another person is different from a conventional soldier who has been deployed by his state prior to an invasion or has fallen into enemy hands following the start of a war. Being part of a large organisation counting tens of thousands of individuals, the conventional soldier is generally a simple instrument directed by a handful of people who are neither aware of the broader plan of the organisation nor in a position to play a role in the activation of threat or aggression. Accordingly, he cannot be considered as having lost his immunity until those leading the entity he is serving have decided to start the aggression, nor can he be considered a threat once he becomes a POW. On the contrary, the smaller nature of terrorist organisations tends to blur the lines between those participating in the attack and those who are planning them. For this reason, the chances are therefore exponentially higher that a terrorist is not only a mere tool but also an active conspirator which also means that his capture does not transform him into a harmless individual because he possesses information about an imminent attack. Contrary to an insurmountable ethical dilemma—such as battlefield mercy killing—when privileging one categorical imperative will inevitably result in the violation of another moral obligation, I would suggest that resorting to VATW or torture against members of a terrorist organisation are *surmountable* dilemmas. However, this does not mean that being able to determine more easily which imperative ought to be favoured ought to give states total *carte blanche*. Their actions must still abide by proper restrictive guidelines, as described in the previous chapter, in which importance consists of not creating situations in which the natural rights of innocent people will end up being harmed. In this regard, the question of torture must follow a similar pattern.

Such an exception is not fundamentally unknown and is usually referred to as a 'defense of necessity,' which is a principle codified in the legal system of many states, such as Article 22 of the Israeli Penal Code. In the case of Germany, although the Constitution explicitly forbids the use of torture or the threat of resorting to torture, the criminal code nonetheless contains a provision that allows state authorities to 'overstep the legally protected interests of the person affected namely, a suspect]' when a there is 'life-threatening danger' to others. This logic of exception bears many similarities with how the whole notion of legitimate defense is conceptually built, and it is as such that we ought to justify torture.

In such cases, 'defense of necessity' is clearly and exclusively connected with the idea of extreme emergencies. For those who defend this idea, it must be mentioned that this scenario is the only possible situation they are envisioning as justifying an exception to the interdiction of torture and not against terrorists who have been captured in a situation where their group is not posing such an imminent threat. Torturing these individuals would simply not be justified as it would not allow states to prevent the death of innocent civilians. Indeed, as argued by Darius Rejali, 'Since World War II, a routine rule of interrogation is that [irregular military] organisations change all critical information within twenty-four to forty-eight hours after its members are arrested (Rejali, 2007, p. 61). Without denying the high value of this objective, it can nonetheless be fulfilled through other alternative ways that do not require torture and opening such a door would be a dangerous slippery slope and an easy expedient for every need to collect intelligence that would take us back to situations like the war in Algeria, where torture became a banal task of interrogators. This has been the claim made in the case of Zaccharias Moussaoui, the so called '20th highjacker of the 9/11 attacks'. Arrested in the weeks before these attacks following a tip from a flying school about his suspicious request of wanting to learn how to pilot a Boeing 747 despite his scant knowledge of flying. After investigating his strange and suspicious practices, he was arrested by the FBI three weeks before the attack and was first held on charges of violating immigration laws. Feeling that Moussaoui's request to the flying school was hiding something bigger, agents requested their supervisors permission to ask for a warrant in order to search his computer. However, as it was later revealed during the 9/11 Commission, this demand was denied because their superiors did not feel that they had sufficient evidence against him to justify a search. As argued by Afsheen John Radsan, 'That is perhaps the tragedy within the tragedy—the lingering thoughts that the catastrophe could have been averted if our officials had better performed their jobs and if the legal structures had not gotten in their way' (2005, p. 1424–1425). What was at stake here was either a lack of proper legal mechanisms that might have justified a search warrant, or simply a lack of proactivity on the part of the FBI. If not searching Moussaoui's computer can be explained by the first reason, then this requires adapting the current laws in light of the terrorist threat to facilitate the granting of search warrants against individuals suspected of this crime. In return, if the lack of action on the part of the authorities was the result of a lack of proactivity of certain members of its intelligence community, then individuals must be held accountable for not fulfilling their tasks properly. However, in both circumstances, none of these reasons may justify resorting to torture. Bureaucratic shortcomings should never form the basis of exceptionalism. If we are to justify the resort to torture, it must be just like VATW, only when no other options are available at our disposal to protect the lives of innocent people.

The main problem with this idea, however, is whether these ticking bomb scenarios are truly empirical or not simply hypothetical situations that have more to do with a Hollywood script than reality. This is a very common criticism, and individuals opposing it argue that reality is always different from theory. Indeed, it lies upon the idea that the individual who has been arrested and against whom torture is being considered is really involved in the crime and that the perceived threat is not only real but also imminent. For Alex Bellamy, this has been the case with what is according to him the one and only ticking bomb scenario state authorities ever had to face in 1957 when the chief of police in Algiers was asked (and refused) to approve the torture of an individual who had been caught planting a bomb, and it was feared that he had planted another one that had yet to be uncovered. Fear of the second bomb was unfounded (2006, p. 141). In this case, this would mean that ticking bomb situations are only fictional and bear no weight with reality and, for this reason, would invalidate the whole discussion as to whether a derogation against resorting to torture ought to be granted.

On this point, it must be said that Bellamy was wrong. Although rare, it is possible to find a few cases of ticking bombs that Bellamy should have been aware of. For instance, four years before he published his text, Germany faced a similar situation that prompted a renewed debate about the morality of torture. In September 2002, a man named Magnus Gäfgen kidnapped an 11-year-old boy and was captured four days after he picked up the ransom he had asked. Knowing that the boy was now alone and that he would only survive a few days, police officers questioned Gäfgen, hoping that he would disclose his location. In light of his refusal to cooperate after four hours of interrogation, fearing that the boy was in imminent danger, the deputy police chief ordered one of his subordinates to resort to whichever measure they believed would make him reveal the boy's location. Two policemen told him that "a specialist" was being flown to Frankfurt by helicopter and that he would "inflict pain on [him] of the sort [he] had never before experienced" (Bernstein, 2003). Faced with this threat, Gäfgen confessed that he had killed the boy and told them about the location of the body. Gäfgen was later found guilty of kidnapping, extortion, and murder (and sentenced to life empowerment), while the deputy chief and his subordinate who threatened Gäfgen of torture were found guilty of instructing a subordinate to commit an offence and coercion.

A similar situation occurred decades before in Florida when Louis Gachelin, a Miami taxi driver, was kidnapped by two individuals, Jean Leon and Frantz Armand, who asked for a ransom of 4,000$. Gachelin's brother, Frank, agreed to meet the abductors and informed the police who followed him secretly to the meeting which led to the arrest of Leon (he was arrested with a gun he drew at Frank Gachelin). It is then that police officers asked Leon to reveal where he was holding Gachelin and was threatened, his arm was twisted behind his back, and he choked after he refused to provide an answer. This abuse led him to finally reveal the location of Gachelin, who was successfully rescued (which also led to the arrest of Armand). These two examples show that real ticking bomb scenarios do actually exist (even if they are in very rare circumstances), which means that the reasonableness of the claim regarding an absolute prohibition of torture must be considered when societies are faced with these sorts of situations.

If we are to summarise the issue at this point, what are the conditions required before resorting to torture against such individuals? As I have already pointed out, it must be only in genuine cases that meet the ticking bomb scenario, that is, when there are no other alternatives at the disposal of police forces to prevent innocent people from being harmed or killed[68] (and I wish to re-emphasise the point that this is the only circumstance where any form of enhanced interrogation may be justified). This obviously comes with the obligation of being able to back up with convincing evidence that and not just mere suspicions that there is indeed an imminent threat that leaves no alternatives to authorities apart from resorting to enhanced techniques of interrogation. Without what can be called these 'evidence', I don't see how torturing an individual would be morally acceptable. The second requirement is derived from what prompted the German police forces to threaten Magnus Gäfgen, inflicting him a sort of pain like he had never experienced before. In this case, it was not just based on the mere suspicion that he had kidnapped the boy, but because he acted in a way that left the inspectors no doubt about his involvement in his kidnapping by picking up the ransom money himself: a suspicion that simply proved itself right after he disclosed the kid's location. Based on this, I would argue that having at one's disposal evidence tends to validate the individual's involvement in the imminent threat. From this perspective, and similarly to the previous condition, there is a need to have information that is convincing enough to support the belief about the individual's participation in the criminal endeavour and his knowledge of it. Of course, genuine cases of ticking bomb scenarios will be scarce, which means that situations where torture could be excused will also be minimised. This is precisely the point at which we ought to think about exceptionalism: the occurrence of such situations should not be common. The next questions that need to be answered are the means that can be employed and how individuals resort to this option ought to justify their decision to do so.

---

68 This was in appearance more obvious in the Gäfgen case than in the one of Louis Gachelin as the former kidnapper explicitly told the police officers that the boy's life was under threat. But this does not make the latter case in comparison less urgent. Indeed, by pulling out a gun when collecting the ransom, Jean Leon proved himself as a very dangerous and determined individual which made the police officers to believe that Louis Gachelin's life was in serious danger. Although all cases of ticking-bomb scenarios are unique, I would argue that these two examples fit its definition.

When it comes to the means that ought to be used against individuals suspected of being knowledgeable about a ticking bomb scenario and how it ought to be justified, there is no doubt that Dershowitz's theory is the most comprehensive and well-known in the literature. Famously known for being the proponent of 'torture warrants', the Harvard law professor is of the opinion that, although illegal, the resort to torture is unfortunately still a common phenomenon throughout the world. If it is obviously more widespread in authoritarian and totalitarian states, it also remains present in democratic societies, as demonstrated by the Gäfgen case as well as in the United States following the 9/11 attacks. Because of this fact, he believes that we ought to find a manner that will allow democratic states to constrain and control this practice whenever they face exceptional circumstances that fit within the framework I have already discussed. In other words, since torture will be used no matter what, he is of the opinion that we ought to improve the situation by thinking about guidelines that would regulate the practice rather than letting low-rank individuals resort secretly to this practice through barbaric means in the basements of police stations or abroad in military bases where domestic laws no longer apply. Unfortunately, this has been the case in the United States over the past 20 years. For instance, it has been reported that:

> American officials acknowledged that such techniques [like sleep and light deprivation and the temporary withholding of food, water, access to sunlight and medical attention] were recently applied as part of the interrogation of Abu Zubaydah, the highest-ranking Al Qaeda operative in custody until the capture of Mr. Mohammed. Painkillers were withheld from Mr. Zubaydah, who was shot several times during his capture in Pakistan. (...) [In another case] Omar al-Faruq, a confidant of Mr. bin Laden and one of Al Qaeda's senior operatives in Southeast Asia, was captured (...) by Indonesian agents acting on a tip from the C.I.A. Agents familiar with the case said a black hood was dropped over his head and he was loaded onto a C.I.A. aircraft. (...) What is known is that the questioning was prolonged, extending day and night for weeks. It is likely, experts say, that the proceedings followed a pattern, with Mr. Faruq left naked most of the time, his hands and feet bound. While international law requires prisoners to be allowed eight hours' sleep a day, interrogators do not necessarily let them sleep for eight consecutive hours. Mr. Faruq may also have been hooked up to sensors, then asked questions to which interrogators knew the answers, so they could gauge his truthfulness, officials said. The Western intelligence official described Mr. Faruq's interrogation as "not quite torture, but about as close as you can get." The official said that over a three-month period, the suspect was fed very little, while being subjected to sleep and light deprivation, prolonged isolation and room temperatures that varied from 100 degrees to 10 degrees. In the end, he began to cooperate (Bonner et al. 2003).

Similarly to what I have argued previously, if torture can ever be excused, it could only occur in genuine cases of ticking bomb scenarios and when there is convincing evidence that strongly suggests that the individual in question is in possession of sensitive information (as in the Leon and Gäfgen cases). This being said, the forms of physical pressure that ought to be tolerated in Dershowitz's perspective should be 'moderate', 'nonlethal' and should not leave permanent physical or psychological trauma. In this regard, he refers to the use of a sterile needle that could be inserted beneath the nails to cause excruciating pain without endangering life or by drilling into a tooth without anaesthesia by trained people and under medical supervision (2004). However, none of this would be allowed without a 'torture warrant' granted by high-level individuals (he mentioned in an interview that this warrant would need to be signed by the Chief Justice following evidence gathered by the Head of State of Head of the Government[69]), who would then be held accountable in the aftermath for their decision. Because these individuals will ultimately have to justify their decision, it is assumed that they will take the proper time to assess the urgency of the situation and whether the evidence is convincing enough to justify a derogation to the normal rules. In his view, this openness to torture would most likely reduce its actual use. He writes:

> [It] seems logical that a formal, visible, accountable, and centralized system is somewhat easier to control than an ad hoc, off-the-books, and under-the radar-screen nonsystem. I believe, though I certainly cannot prove, that a formal requirement of a judicial warrant as a prerequisite to nonlethal torture would decrease the amount of physical violence directed against suspects. At the most obvious level, a double check is always more protective than a single check. In every instance in which a warrant is requested, a field officer has already decided that torture is justified and, in the absence of a warrant requirement, would simply proceed with the torture. Requiring that decision to be approved by a judicial officer will result in fewer instances of torture even if the judge rarely turns down a request. Moreover, I believe that most judges would require compelling evidence before they would authorize so extraordinary a departure from our constitutional norms, and law enforcement officials would be reluctant to seek a warrant unless they had compelling evidence that the suspect had information needed to prevent an imminent terrorist attack (2002, pp. 158–159).

Although this argument can be (and has been) criticized (Allhoff, 2011), the main problem with Dershowitz thesis is the fact that he believes that torture cannot begin until these warrants have been granted. The main and obvious problem lies with its chronology, which is utterly impractical in the case of ticking bomb scenarios where the time to act may be too limited to follow Dershowitz's protocol, which requires the approval of the highest state officials. It is easy to assume that providing these individuals with the details of the case and allowing them enough time to assess the evidence will take time if we wish the procedure

---

69 https://www.youtube.com/watch?v=M4sduqzV_1U

to be thorough and not expeditive to avoid committing a judicial error that would result in the torture of an innocent person. Although perfectly sound in my mind, an essential component of Dershowitz's thesis—namely, the process leading to the granting of a torture warrant—simply makes it unpracticable in cases (ticking bomb scenarios), it is supposed to apply to. What to do then? Abandon the proposal for exceptional treatment of certain individuals who qualify as terrorists? If this were to be the case, it would end up violating the state's categorical imperative to protect the lives of its citizens. The only alternative would be to allow police officers the right to torture prior to getting a warrant, but by establishing a process that would require them, in the aftermath, to be held accountable for their decision. This would consist of an open enquiry during which the evidence that led them to conclude that they were facing a ticking bomb scenario and that torturing the suspect(s) was the only solution to save lives. They ought to know in return that failure to demonstrate that the situation was indeed urgent and that the evidence against the suspect(s) was convincing enough exposed them to harsh legal consequences.

In conclusion, the uniqueness of terrorism and its *modus operandi* pressures states in an ethical dilemma that bears no similarities with the treatment of conventional soldiers. This tension has been directly linked to the use of torture (or of 'enhanced interrogation techniques') by certain liberal democracies. Although not an easy question to address, it remains in my opinion that having to choose between saving the lives of innocent people over causing deliberate harm to a defenceless individual is not insurmountable and the reason being; despite having been arrested, he remains an active threat in cases of ticking bomb scenarios. As such, this captured terrorist has more in common with a conventional soldier, who has not surrendered his weapons. Therefore, this creates an intermediary category of combatants between those who are not POW (and who can accordingly be killed) and those who have been captured or who are not involved in a ticking bomb scenario (and who should not be harmed in any way). Because of their 'captured/yet still posing an active threat' status, the ethical dilemma is not an absolute one where whatever decision is made will inevitably result in the violation of another deontological moral rule.

Chapter 5
Can Terrorism be Used in Exceptional Circumstances?

After all that has previously been said, the third and last ethical dilemma associated with terrorism is whether or not the violation of one categorical imperative, that is, whether resorting to terrorism by deliberately harming those who
qualify as non-combatants can ever be justified for the sake of putting an end
to war and thereby preventing further deaths and destruction. As has already
been argued in the preceding chapters, because of its inherent violation of
men's most important natural rights, that is, the right to life, the use of political
violence against other human beings needs some serious justifications. It is generally accepted that individuals lose immunity against being harmed or killed
when they pose a threat to other people. When this is the case, those facing menace enjoy the right of self-defense. Not only is this applicable to the domestic
laws of countries around the world, but it is also how the justification of killing
during wartime is largely justified (Walzer, 2006; McMahan, McMahan, 2004;
McPherson, 2004) as well and guerrilla warfare insofar as the conditions discussed in the second chapter are met. This is why terrorism, which is the indiscriminate targeting of people, is seen as being highly problematic, since it necessarily implies that individuals who have not engaged in moral responsibility in
a criminal endeavour will inevitably end up being killed alongside those who
have. There are nonetheless many people who have made that claim and that terror as a war measure can sometimes be justified when it is deemed to serve a
higher moral end, such as accelerating the end of a conflict (as it was the
case with the Hiroshima and Nagasaki bombings) or in order to prevent evil
from triumphing (an idea that refers to Michael Walzer's doctrine of 'supreme
emergency'). What is the aim of such a claim? Despite its inherent morality, terrorism can nonetheless be justified in certain situations. This is discussed in this
chapter.

Determining someone's guilt for a wrongdoing is usually proportional to the extent of one's participation in a crime and his knowledge (as well as his capacity
to become aware) of any wrongdoing being perpetrated. In this regard, the more
distant a person becomes from the knot of the decision-making process, the less
he or she engages his or her personal responsibility in any wrongdoing. Similarly, the more a person becomes a victim of invincible ignorance, the more exempt
he or she can be from any guilt. In this sense, it is problematic to talk about any-

https://doi.org/10.1515/9783110757569-006

thing other than individual guilt, which is why trying to justify the deliberate targeting of random people on the basis that they are collectively guilty as members of what is deemed by terrorists as a 'criminal political entity' is problematic. However, we must be aware that if this logic was ever justified, then it would lead to the possibility of legitimising terrorism in the same way that the resort to guerrilla warfare can be morally acceptable. Therefore, it is important to thoroughly analyse this prospect.

Following WWII, German philosopher Karl Jaspers famously wrote in his book *The Question of German Guilt* that no German was guilty of the atrocities committed by the Nazi regime (2000, p. 16). This was and is still a strong assumption worth debating since, as I have argued previously, the nature of Hitler's rule would have rightfully justified its victims, mainly the Jews, defending themselves as a matter of self-defense. Fighting off the final solution would have justified their resort to violence from a moral standpoint. As a consequence of this, and because all Germans were considered by Jaspers to be collectively guilty of their regime's hideous crimes, does this mean that victims of the latter would have been justified to resort to the indiscriminate killing of the former which would not have been considered a crime because none of them were non-innocent?

Jaspers' assessment of guilt and liability can be answered in four ways: 1. the criminal guilt, 2. political guilt; and 3. the moral guilt and 4. the metaphysical guilt. Criminal guilt is defined as the result of specific crimes committed by certain individuals who violate national and international laws. For instance, an individual who is ordering a violation of Article 2 (4) of the UN Charter is guilty of what the judges of the Nuremberg Trials labelled a crime against peace; an individual who is purposedly targeting innocent civilians during wartime is guilty of a war crime, while those who are actively involved in the mass murder of individuals based on their religion, ethnicity, or race are for their part guilty of crimes against humanity. Jaspers defines political guilt as the responsibility of citizens for the immoral and illegal deeds committed by their state, while moral guilt concerns individuals who must answer their own conscience for having lived with a guilty conscience about the deeds committed by their state but who nonetheless chose to stay silent and refused to oppose them actively[70]. Lastly, metaphysical guilt is defined 'as the lack of "absolute solidarity with the human being as such" and found its expression in the feeling of guilt at being

---

70 Jaspers writes about this type of guilt that it includes '(...) the ones who knew, or could know, and yet walked in ways which self-analysis reveals to them as culpable error-whether conveniently closing their eyes to events, or permitting themselves to be intoxicated, seduced or bought with personal advantages, or obeying from fear' (p. 56–57).

alive when one's Jewish neighbors were being taken away' (Taylor Wilkins, 1992, p. 14).

For Jaspers, it is clear that guilts 1, 3 and 4 are either individual by nature or derivative of other people's actions with whom we are connected, it would be 'nonsensical to charge a whole people for these crimes' (Jaspers, 2000, p. 34). It is individual when some people are purposely acting unlawfully, such as soldiers who are choosing not to abide in accordance with the Geneva Conventions by torture or killing POW. It is also the result of other people's actions with whom we are linked in some peculiar ways, whether through contracts or in a hierarchical manner. More precisely, by transferring some of our responsibilities from our own will to others, we remain entirely responsible for illegal actions made on our behalf. For instance, by blindly trusting an accountant to do my taxes, I remain liable to the tax authorities if he or she is purposely or by mistake not reporting all my earnings or not paying to the state the sum of money I may owe. Liability can also be attributed to individuals who are in a situation of authority with regard to the actions their subordinates have taken. This is the case with what is referred to as 'command responsibility' in the military and implies that those in command have certain obligations to ensure that their men serving under their authority will act lawfully. This implies a type of proactivity that expands beyond the simple occasional reminder that subordinates have to respect the moral rules of warfare. Indeed, this means assessing personal situations when the possibility of crimes being committed exists and launching any investigations whenever they are hearing rumours or are presented with evidence that crimes have been committed by their men. For instance, when a commander is informed that his unit has taken POW, the possibility of their mistreatments must be entertained, which is why he must display proactive measures and actions that will prevent these violations of warfare rules from occurring. This may take the form of visiting the POW on a regular basis and talking to them. In return, any suspicion that their rights may have been violated ought to lead him to launch a formal enquiry and eventually punish those who may have been responsible for them. However, this type of liability is unidirectional and does not apply to subordinates when a crime has been committed by those who are above them in the hierarchy or the chain of command, since it is assumed that the former have no possible way of controlling the actions of the latter or are unable to suspect that their actions are facilitating the unlawful endeavours of their boss. More precisely, stock brokers who are simply doing their jobs cannot be held accountable for their CEO's decision to steal money from the company.

On the other hand, the second type of guilt is thought by jaspers to be inherently collective and affects every member of a given state, even those who opposed the regime's illegal activities (p. 34). His reasons are that by letting an un-lawful and immoral regime rise among them through voting (or by failing to vote), political liability for the crimes of a state 'lets no man dodge'[71] (p. 56). For Joel Feinberg, this type of collective guilt resembles the following situation.

> Consider the case of the Jesse James train robbery. One armed man holds up an entire car full of passengers. If the passengers had risen up as one man and rushed at the robber, one or two of them would have overwhelmed him, disarmed him, and saved their property. Yet they all meekly submitted. How responsible were they for their own losses? Not very. In a situation like this, only heroes could be expected to lead the sacrificial charge, so no indi-vidual in the group was at fault for not resisting. The whole group, however, had it within its power to resist successfully (1970, p. 248).

In return, we cannot say the same about passengers of United Airlines flight 93 who took upon themselves to charge the cockpit of the plane in order to prevent bin Laden's men from crashing it against U.S. Capitol. At the expense of their lives, these heroes were able to prevent greater harm and once could only won-der if a sufficient number of Germans had done the same in 1933, Hitler may not have been able to establish a viable dictatorship.

What is Jaspers' approach to collective responsibility? With all due respect, I believe that it lies upon a grossly inaccurate assessment of guilt that depends on an essentialist conception of communities that ignores individual choices and preferences, as well as an unreasonable expectation of how humans ought to be-have. Consequently, it can hardly support the terrorist logic that the indiscrimi-nate targeting of people can be justified. Collective responsibility exists in situa-tions where a fault has not been committed by all members of an organisation or a joint endeavour. For instance, it is a well-known fact that 'there is no 'I' in team', which is why all members of a hockey team who have been on the starting lineup during the playoffs will equally be able to have their name engraved on the Stanley Cup and to receive their ring if their team ends up winning the cham-pionship. They are all collectively considered to be responsible for the success of

---

71 Jaspers goes on to add that: 'If things go wrong the politically active tend to justify them-selves; but such defenses carry no weight in politics. For instance, they meant well and had the best intentions—Hindenburg, for one, did surely not mean to ruin Germany or hand it over to Hitler. That does not help him; he did—and that is what counts. Or they foresaw the dis-aster, said so, and warned; but that does not count politically, either, if no action followed or if it had no effect. One might think of cases of wholly non-political persons who live aloof of all pol-itics, like monks, hermits, scholars, artists-if really quite non-political, those might possibly be excused from all guilt. Yet they, too, are included among the politically liable, because they, too, live by the order of the state. There is no such aloofness in modern states' (p. 56).

their team and, in return, will also bear a similar view of themselves if they end up losing championship. In this case, they will all say 'that the collective did not deliver' or that 'they did not display the collective strength needed to win'. Of course, it is always possible to say that one player made a crucial mistake that ended up costing the victory, but one play does not erase the other opportunities that other members of the team may have missed previously during the game. In such cases, blame is never an individual but collective. However, can we translate this analogy into the actions of a state?

The reason for this is that the sports example lies upon a very strong understanding of solidarity, which has no similarities with the relationships between people in a political community. Indeed, in a hockey team, all players and supporting staff are unquestionably espousing the same objective/ideal (i.e. to win the championship) and are all fully dedicated to fulfilling this task during the whole season. Those whose dedication or talent is deemed not at the required level are traded, sent back to the minor leagues, invited to watch the games from the stands, or are having their contract terminated. This reality is entirely different in a state where citizens share different conceptions of what they should achieve collectively (as is clearly exemplified by the diversity of votes during an election). Supporting an opposite view by asserting the same strong idea of solidarity that defines smaller organisations like sports teams to millions of people who simply happen to be governed by the same entity would negate their individuality and to assign them an overarching 'collective spirit' that takes precedence over their personal choices. This is an anti-democratic assessment of societies that would ultimately negate individual freedom. I will not go down that road. In this sense, we can wonder how legitimate it is to put some sort of blame on citizens for the unlawful crimes that they have actively and openly criticised.

To return to the sport example, some people might say that these citizens should have done like French cyclist Christophe Bassons, who openly criticised mass doping during the 1999 Tour de France and who, disgusted with what his beloved sport had become, simply chose to leave the professional peloton. In return, those who silently shared his views but nonetheless decided not to severe ties with their team contributed to the *status quo* and to a situation that ultimately led to the voiding of results more than 10 years after Bassons' initial accusations. Many would argue that these cyclists share a collective blame for their pursued collaboration with their sport, despite their disagreements with widespread doping practices. If they would have joined Bassons in his denunciation, maybe the *Union cycliste internationale,* the sport's governing body, would have acted or team sponsors, and TV networks would have threatened to terminate their collaboration with race and grand tour organisers, thereby killing cycling as a profession or forcing massive changes to it. Perhaps these clean cyclists can at least claim today not to have been guilty of cheating by injecting banned substances into their bodies, but their silence contributed to the ethical necrosis of their sport. In the same vein, can we say that citizens who are deceived by one of their state policies that have led to the commitment of crimes who nonetheless chose not to go in exile and keep on paying their taxes every year share the same guilt as the gutless cyclists who did not follow Bassons' footsteps by leaving the sport? This is Jaspers' view which is in my view inherently wrong, because it is not possible to link people with their government as if they were forming a monistic group which, as a consequence, can only lead them to be treated in a totalitarian manner. Political associations are more complicated than sports teams.

The difference between these two situations is people's genuine capacity to choose severe ties with the entity they perceive as following an inappropriate path. In the case of a sport, individuals do not face undue obstacles. They can simply terminate their contracts with their teams and move on to their lives. Of course, they will have to find another way to pay the bills, but this is not an impossible task and will most likely not lead to their death by starvation because of the numerous social programs in place in liberal democracies. This is, of course, not the case with an individual dissatisfied with his state, whose capacity to do so depends on his capacity to leave his country (which may not be the case if it is an authoritarian or totalitarian regime) and, second, to be able to live abroad in a country that may be willing to grant him asylum and, lastly, his capacity to financially support himself (and his family) with his new life. Furthermore, being able to leave may also imply leaving behind family members, who could then face the consequences of their exile. In other words, there is much more at stake in this second case, which justifies why opponents who decide to stay in their country, despite their disagreements with their policies, cannot be held responsible for their continuous involvement with their entity. Contrary to cyclists, breaking ties is not solely a matter of willingness. What is expected of citizens is, in this case, heroism (just like in the Jesse James example), and I simply find it difficult to blame individuals for refusing to act in a way which is considered to be above and beyond what is expected from a human being. Even in a democratic state, justifying someone's guilt on the basis that he is paying taxes to his state ignores the fact that refusing to do so implies serious legal consequences that may lead to jailtime. Criticising individuals and assigning them guilt for trying to avoid being sent to prison is simply not a reasonable expectation to entertain. In addition, we may say that their continuous political involvement is a matter of duress, especially in authoritarian and totalitarian regimes, a legal reality that absolves individuals of any wrongdoings (Caron 2018). Knowing that actively denouncing a policy may lead individuals to be arrested, tortured, and sentenced to disproportionate punishment[72], asking them to show any form of dissidence is akin to suicide. In this sense, arguing that not participating in an anti-regime protest makes them liable for their state's crime is nothing more than moral fundamentalism, which is completely disconnected from reality. Even asserting that having been present at a party rally or for having raised one's right arm while screaming at the same time 'Heil Hitler' makes someone liable for the crimes of their state problematic, especially in situations when a lack of proactive display of support for the leader, his party, and the state are perceived as signs of hostility or counter-revolutionary behaviour (i.e. terrible consequences on one's freedom and life)[73].

As a consequence, we can assume that everybody in a sports team is collectively liable for its failure or success actively because they are either clearly expressing support for its objective or by making the decision to support it silently despite their discomfort with the way it is being pursued. This is why the decision of grand tour organisers to eject or not to grant invitations to entire cycling teams when one of their riders is caught for doping is justified, as this type of cheating can hardly be kept away from everyone in the team because it usually requires the support and collaboration of numerous individuals, as was the case with the Festina affair of 1997. When this is the case, individuals are either active or silent participants, and the latter are in these circumstances as guilty as the former are. On the other hand, refusing to leave one's country and to keep paying taxes that will in part serve to finance its murderous and criminal deeds does not entail the same liability. Because their continuous political involvement can be the result of 'forced voluntarism', these individuals ought to remain free of any political guilt. In this case, if the indiscriminate treatment of all members of a cycling team can be justified, this cannot be the case with every citizen of a state pursuing an unlawful path.

If we were to equalise political guilt with the indiscriminate loss of immunity against being harmed or killed, not only would it be required to justify how it applies equally to everybody, but also that this guilt justifies the loss of immunity. There is simply no need to talk about the latter consequence—which would require some serious justifications as to why death ought to be required for active

---

72 As in Russia for instance where, following the invasion of Ukraine, the Parliament adopted a law that prescribes up to 15 years in prison for individuals who are disseminating 'false information' about the conflict.

73 It is important here to recall Saint-Just's quote mentioned in chapter 1 according to which punishing inactive citizens and those not actively showing their support for the Revolution was justified. When this is the case, even an active support for an unlawful policy can be seen as a result of duress.

participants in a state's crime (as can be done following what has been argued in Chapter 2) as well as against individuals whose continuous political involvement with a state is forced, because it is simply not possible to justify indiscriminate guilt. Those opposing a state's crime through violence would then be required to find ways to target random individuals who are not opponents of the state policy. Unfortunately, for them, individuals' political choices are not tattooed on their forehead, and bombs cannot be programmed to only target supporters of a regime and miraculously protect political opponents.

Moreover, we also need to consider that individuals living in these regimes are also the victims of their state propaganda and, as a consequence, their support for their state may be the result of their altered and manipulated mind and, as a result, can hardly be blamed for it, just as it would not be reasonable to punish an individual committing a crime while under hypnosis. In this sense, if we were to argue that all Germans were guilty—from a political Jasperian perspective— to allow the rise of Hitler to power and, accordingly, all deserved to be targeted by their victims, we could easily say that this culpability did not extend beyond themselves. Indeed, in a situation where the lack of heroism of a few leads to the establishment of a criminal state that can only lead to the 'banality of evil' (to take Arendt's expression) and to the eradication of individuals' personality and rational capacities to distinguish between what is morally acceptable from what is not thanks to the efforts of state's propaganda. If the adults who witnessed Hitler's or the Kim's family tree rose to power in Germany and in North Korea could be held politically guilty, it would be difficult to assert the same for their children and grandchildren who, as a result of the establishment of these totalitarian regimes, were brainwashed into thinking about the inferiority of the Jews or the Juche ideology. Their support for their respective regime and lack of anti-regime activism could therefore not be perceived as their wilful decision, but as a forced one, hereby adding another layer of difficulty for those victims of these regimes in determining who ought to be rightfully harmed through guerrilla warfare.

We can therefore conclude that justifying the indiscriminate targeting of people on the basis that individuals are collectively guilty[74] of crimes committed by one's state is untenable. Guiltiness that justifies a loss of immunity against harm and death can hardly extend beyond the scope already discussed in Chapter 2, at the risk of justifying the assassination of individuals who have not engaged in their personal responsibility in a state crime. Such a justification would result

---

74 Whichis no longer indiscriminate since that notion lies upon a distinction between the guilty and the innocents. When everybody is deemed to be guilty, this notion no longer makes sense.

in considering terrorism as a form of political violence based on what I have already described as moral fundamentalism, which refuses to assess the imperfect nature of human beings and the political realities that make them acting in a heroic way hardly possible.

Despite these difficulties in justifying terroristic methods according to this view of collective responsibility, there is still a tendency to argue that they can remain acceptable. In this case, their justifiability is not based on the fact that people ought to be targeted, because they have engaged in their moral responsibility in the inhumane actions of their government. Rather, it finds roots in the desire to serve a higher good. In this regard, the whole question consists of determining the circumstances under which this can be justified.

If terrorism is defined as the deliberate targeting of civilians for political purposes, one needs to wonder if there are circumstances where resorting to this tactic can be morally justified for the sake of serving a higher good, such as putting an end to war and establishing peace. In this regard, the best example that comes to mind are the bombings of Hiroshima and Nagasaki in 1945 that broke Japan's will to fight and forced the country into surrendering a few days later. One thing is for sure however: if these bombings were ever morally justifiable, it is certainly not because the citizens of these two cities had lost their immunity against harm and death[75]. The justification must lie elsewhere, and the whole question is therefore what it could be.

It must be noted that the just war theory already has a way to justify the harm of innocent people as a side effect of promoting a good end. Known as the doctrine of the double effect, this idea permits violation of the principle of discrimination when it results from the targeting of a military objective. According to this principle, an air force would be justified to bomb a factory where tanks are assembled, even though the operation would very likely result in the killing of civilians living in its vicinity. What can be labelled in this case as a 'strategic bombing' should therefore not be confused with 'terror bombing' and the former is unfortunately a necessary notion to consider since it is basically impossible to envisage fighting in environments that are entirely deprived of civilians (with the exceptions of the sea, deserts or maybe one day in space). It would indeed be naive to think of war as a reality that would restrict death

---

75 Walzer writes about this so-called justification that: 'How did the people of Hiroshima [and Nagasaki] forfeit their rights? Perhaps their taxes paid for some of the ships and planes used in the attack on Pearl Harbor; perhaps they sent their sons into the navy and air force with prayers for their success; perhaps they celebrated the actual event, after being told that their country had won a great victory in the face of an imminent American threat. Surely there is nothing here that makes these people liable to direct attack' (Walzer, 2006, p. 264).

solely to combatants, and it is accordingly a necessity to have a way of distinguishing war crimes from civilians' death as the result of collateral damage.

Needless to say however, the willingness to destroy a legitimate military target does not necessarily mean that states are entitled to use any means at their disposal to achieve their aim. If this were to be the case, the doctrine of the double effect would be far too lenient and would end up justifying any humanitarian tragedy on the basis that it was not intended. To avoid falling into this trap, combatants must find ways to minimise unintended impacts on the principle of discrimination. This is why Walzer believes (rightfully I think) that this idea, which he refers to as the 'double intention' criterion, must be added to the principle of double effect. Not doing that would easily blur the lines between a state's rightful ways of waging war and state terrorism. More specifically, the notion of double intention may imply using weapons whose known and expected impacts will be as proportionate as possible with the targeted aim, applying proper rules of engagement similar to those previously discussed regarding the use of drones, as well as requiring combatants to make positive commitments to save civilian lives even if it means increasing the risks for themselves up to a point where the risks taken are not to be considered as suicidal (Caron, 2018, pp. 93–106)[76].

Of course, this discussion is only a short summary of what the doctrine of the double effect is about and how it can be supplemented by additional requirements that aim to ensure a better respect for the moral rules of warfare. However, as a highly complex topic, it is not surprising that it has led to numerous debates in the literature (Predelli, 2004; Lee, 2004; Buzar, 2020). Without wanting to ignore these very important debates (because they are important), my intention is rather to question in the following pages whether terror bombing (i. e. the voluntary indiscriminate targeting of civilians) can be justified when it serves a higher purpose. In this regard, we often think of the bombings of Hiroshima and Nagasaki as quintessential examples of actions that led to the death of tens of thou-

---

76 In this regard, Walzer provides several examples in *Just and Unjust Wars*, such as the one of the bombing of occupied France by the Free France air force. He writes: 'During World War II, the Free France air force carried out bombing raids against military targets in occupied France. Inevitably, their bombs killed Frenchmen working (under coercion) for the German war effort; inevitably too, they killed Frenchmen who simply happened to live in the vicinity of the factories under attack. This posed a cruel dilemma for the pilots, which they resolved not by giving up the raids or asking someone else to carry them out, but by accepting greater risks for themselves. 'It was (...) this persistent question of bombing France itself', says Pierre Mendes-France, who served in the air force after his escape from a German prison, 'which led us to specialize more and more in precision bombing—that is, flying at a very low altitude. It was more risky, but it also permitted greater precision' (2006, p. 157).

sands of individuals[77] in order to force Japan into surrendering and saving the lives of at least half a million American soldiers who might have died as a result of the invasion of Japan[78]. Instead of answering whether these bombings were morally acceptable or defendable, historians mostly focused on whether they were necessary. In this regard, it has been argued that Japan's defeat occurred in the summer of 1945. Its navy had already been at that time sunk for the most part, the country's fuel reserves were running dry, its troops in China were effectively cut off from Tokyo, and its major cities were bombed night after night by the US B-29 bombers. Furthermore, because the Japanese secret coding system had already been broken, President Truman was aware that many members of the Japanese government were willing to accept a negotiated peace pending on the condition that the Americans would not remove Emperor Hiro-Hito from the Chrysanthemum Throne (which was ultimately granted by the Americans even though they were initially pressured for an unconditional surrender). The bombings of Hiroshima and Nagasaki most likely simply accelerated Japan's decision to lay down its arms, but resorting to this terrorist mean was clearly not, contrary to what has been said, the only option since the Japanese-only demand was considered acceptable. We can therefore presuppose that ending the war could have been achieved without resorting to the bombings of Hiroshima and Nagasaki.

However, beyond this debate, the moral question remains unanswered: Was resorting to this act of terrorism morally defendable? We should not be afraid to say that it was an act of terrorism for the reasons evoked in 1963 in a judgment from a Japanese tribunal that came to the obvious conclusion that these bombings were clear violations of the laws and customs of war because the attacks were deliberately indiscriminate and did not distinguish between military and civilian targets (Shimoda et al. v. the State, 1963).

Members of Truman's cabinet justified them on the basis of a utilitarian logic articulated around the idea that if they had not used these bombs, the US air force would have done the worst and would have caused more deaths. Indeed, Americans had already started months before the mass indiscriminate bombings of large cities with incendiary devices that killed tens of thousands of civilians

---

[77] Based on the most conservative accounts, these two bombs killed at least 50,000 people respectively. To this number, we also need to add those wounded by the attacks who died a few weeks later, but also those who felt victims of the radiations in the years that followed. In fact, we will never know for sure how many people died as a result of these two bombings.
[78] President Harry Truman declared after he left the White House that he had used the atomic bomb to save the lives of half a million or even a million American boys who might have died in an island-by-island battle to the bitter end for the conquest of Japan (Powers, 1995).

(in the case of Tokyo in March 1945, the estimate is that around 100,000 people were killed). Knowing that using the atomic bomb would have been as murderous as resorting to conventional bombings, the US Secretary of War and State Secretary were of the opinion that its tremendous psychological impact would force the Japanese into submission; something the use of incendiary bombs was not allowed to achieve. In other words, their claim was that they were allowed to breach a little bit the moral rules of warfare and increase the level of terror so that they would not have to break them on a larger scale. In other words, little harm ought to be better than bigger harm. However, this logic is flawed because it does not question whether the harm is in itself acceptable (in this case, causing the death of tens of thousands of civilians) and, in this sense, the antithesis of what war ought to be all about. If it is ever accepted as a justified reason for targeting civilians, terrorists would then have the capacity to justify the high jacking and crash of a plane filled with innocent people by saying that it was ultimately less deadly than a bomb planted in a football stadium on a Sunday afternoon (or that they could have done worst, like using a dirt bomb in a crowded downtown area). This would obviously mean walking on dangerous grounds.

Of course, it may also be possible to argue that these bombings were ordered in accordance with the principle of double effect, despite the fact that they were highly lethal for non-combatants. Indeed, they were driven by a highly valuable and acceptable objective: to stop the war and prevent the death of hundreds of thousands of American soldiers (as well as those of Japanese soldiers and civilians who would have died during the invasion). In this case, the deliberate targeting of civilians living in these two sacrificed cities was not the intended objective, but rather collateral victims. Moreover, not only were the killing of civilians not their intended aim, but the positive effects that resulted from them compensated for their negative consequences. In fact, justifying these bombings is probably the best possible example of Henry Sidgwick's proposed view of how wars ought to be fought. Relying on utilitarianism, Sidgwick believes that the whole purpose of war is to win it as quickly as possible and, as a consequence, would consider every action that can play a significant part in this regard as licit and acceptable[79]. This was clearly the case with the Hiroshima and Nagasaki bombings, since Japan announced its intention to surrender six days after the latter bombing. However, and as I have argued previously, isolating the principle of double effect from any other ethical considerations (such as

---

79 Summarizing Sidgwick's view, Michael Walzer writes in this regard: 'Hence anything should be permitted that is useful and proportionate to the victory being sought' (2006, pp. 130–131).

the 'double intention' criterion) is problematic as it would simply elevate the 'winning the war objective' as the sole criterion soldiers ought to think about, hereby opening the door wide open for justifying terroristic methods as banal and acceptable realities of warfare. Indeed, this objective can be used in such a generous way that any battle can be deemed strategic for the war effort, with the result that all actions would first and foremost end up subjecting the expectation to 'fight well' to the imperative of victory. In return, we cannot ignore the fact that this logic would at the end of the day also provide ample justifications to terrorist organizations in their own use of indiscriminate means of warfare that they would perceive as essential for the victory of the cause they are fighting for. By placing the whole emphasis on achieving victory at the end of the day, this utilitarian logic would lead every camp to openly embrace without any remorse barbarian methods of warfare whenever they would be deemed favourable to the achievement of their ultimate objective. This is simply not an acceptable way to justify terroristic means of fighting.

Another way of justifying these bombings could be through the prism of the United States fighting a moral war after it had been treacherously attacked at Pearl Harbor on 7 December 1941 and was simply upholding its inherent right to self-defense. For that reason, some may be tempted to argue that 'The greater the justice of my cause, the more rules I can violate for the sake of the cause' (Walzer, 2006, p. 229). In a nutshell, this was another part of President Truman's decision to order the bombings of Hiroshima and Nagasaki (alongside the utilitarian calculation that it would end the war)[80]. This has been the view held by many people and mass media during the recent war in Ukraine, who have forgiven the violations to the Geneva Conventions that Ukrainian troops have perpetrated against Russian POWs[81] more easily than those committed by Russian soldiers against Ukrainians. This is a natural and perfectly understandable phenomenon to side with the victim over the aggressor, but abiding by this logic simply ends up being an open door for the rejection of any possibility to limit wartime violence solely to a limited number of individuals who have lost immun-

---

80 In his August 12, 1945, speech, he said the following: 'We have used [the bomb] against those who attacked us without warning at Pearl Harbor, against those who have starved and beaten and executed American prisoners of war, against those who have abandoned all pretense of obeying international laws of warfare. We have used it in order to shorten the agony of war' (Walzer, 2006, p. 264).

81 Images have indeed shown Ukrainian soldiers shoot Russian POWs in the legs or kill wounded combatants who had their hands tied behind their back.

ity against harm and death[82]. Even in domestic laws, the right to self-defense does not provide its beneficiary with a full licence over what he is entitled to do to repel the attack. Consequently, this is not an option that ought to be entertained to justify the resort to terroristic means of fighting. In fact, holding the view that the one fighting for a just cause ought to enjoy the right to use whatever means he feels necessary to win the war is a slippery slope that can easily lead us to shift from the 'just war logic' in favour of one that is more connected with an idea of 'moral war'. If the former approach seeks to justify the morality of warfare both from the *jus ad bellum* and *jus in bello* categories, the latter is, for its part, embracing a single criterion, which is the morality of the cause we are fighting for. This notion is considered sufficient in itself to assess the rightness of a war fought by a state or any other entity, thereby erasing the obligation to fight well. Indeed, and as has been argued by French philosopher Monique Canto-Sperber, violence exercised for the sake of a higher good, whether for the eradication of a murderous ideology or to make freedom and democracy triumph, is violence that can hardly be moderate because of the absolute nature of its objective that is not open to compromises (2010, pp. 40–41). In this sense, war and violence are becoming simple means to achieve a desirable good, and the legitimacy of warfare primarily lies upon the identity of who is fighting rather than the way they are fighting. This logic has, therefore, a lot in common with St. Augustine's idea of 'benevolent severity,' which lies on the belief that any type of harm is excusable whenever it is animated by a sincere desire to achieve good.

   This is why Walzer argued that this logic should only apply to exceptional situations when it could be said that victory is so important and the prospect of defeat so terrifying that it could be legitimate to ignore the moral rules of warfare. This is what he refers to as situations of 'supreme emergencies' against enemies at a time when their imminent victory poses an existential threat to mankind. Without any surprises, the example he is using—and it is unfortunately his only one—to talk about such outstanding situations is that of the Nazis and the allies resorting to the terroristic mass indiscriminate bombings of German cities during WWII. To qualify for this exception, these two requisites are essential: the moral identity of our foe and his imminent victory. When one of them is lacking, states must return to actions and strategies that abide by the moral rules of warfare. In this sense, if these bombings may have been justified (more about the

---

82 This is also Walzer's view on the matter when he writes : 'the extreme form of the sliding-scale argument is the claim that soldiers fighting a just war can do anything at all that is useful in the fighting. This effectively annuls the war convention and denies or suspends the rights that the convention was designed to protect. The war rights of the just are total, and any blame their actions entail falls upon the leaders of the other side' (Walzer, 2006, p. 230).

discussion in the following pages) after Great Britain was left fighting Hitler alone after June 1940, they should have stopped after it became clear that Germany was inevitably going to lose war[83], which was not the case and why, as mentioned in the first chapter. In a way, the doctrine of supreme emergency must be understood as an ethical paradox when acting in one way or another will always imply violating another moral rule, which is why it probably should not be formally codified as being legal, but instead recognised as merely excusable when the actor resorting to it is able to provide a convincing rationale for the justification of his actions (Orend, 2013; Cook, 2007)[84].

What should be considered in this approach? Many criticisms have been addressed of Walzer (Lund, 2011; Neu, 2013; Toner, 2005) with one of them being the capacity to clearly identify a truly immoral enemy. Indeed, it is well known that states facing defeat will always tend to demonise their foe and claim that their victory is morally required. This almost constant call tends to make the exceptionalism of the supreme emergency rather a banal reality that ends up blurring the lines between states that are facing a true urgency from those that are not.

Another problem with Walzer's thesis relates to how he links his doctrine with his understanding of the meaning of a political community. He writes in *Arguing About War* that a supreme emergency exists when a 'community is threatened, not just in its present territorial extension or governmental structure or prestige or honour, but in what [its people] might think of as its *ongoingness* (...)' and when its enemy is threatening to end its collective way of life, that is, the communal practices and principles that define it (Walzer, 2004, p. 43). According to this view, the British resort to the terrorist bombings of German cities was based on the assumption that they had the right to do so because the Nazis were trying to eradicate another civilizational conception of mankind, thereby preventing people living in European liberal democracies from having the capacity to carry on with their own distinctive way of life and hand it down to

---

83 Pinpointing that precise moment is of course very difficult. In retrospect, we may say that it was June 22, 1941, after Germany made the fatal mistake of declaring war against USSR. We could also say December 1941 when the United States with its incomparable might joined the war. More conservatively, I would argue that the beginning of 1943 was really the turning point of the war following the defeat of Rommel's Afrikakorps in Northern Africa (which then allowed a few weeks later the allies to land in Sicily) as well as the capitulation of Field Marshall Friedrich von Paulus 6th Army in Stalingrad. From that point on, the question was no longer if Germany would be defeated, but when it would be forced to surrender.

84 Even Walzer himself seems to abide by this logic when he writes that 'overriding the rules leaves guilt behind, as a recognition of the enormity of what we have done and a commitment not to make our actions into an easy precedent for the future' (2004, p. 34).

their children and grandchildren. This view lies in the conviction that the mere disappearance of social or civilizational principles and values would be of great harm to its members. It is argued that having a common culture has always been instrumental in achieving its essential functions (Caron, 2021bcd). Sharing a language and history generates a strong bond between millions of unknown individuals, and this sense of a common identity and membership generates among such individuals the willingness to make sacrifices for each other. This common culture also facilitates the integration of individuals through the same 'shared vocabulary of tradition and convention' (Kymlicka, 1995, p. 77). Historically, immigrants have been expected to assimilate into their new culture—a process that has been encouraged through various means, such as the high bureaucratisation of all aspects of people's lives that has forced newcomers to abide by the official state language and public schooling, which facilitates the full integration of the children of immigrants. Depending on these institutional tools, culture is doomed to disappear. Because of the pervasiveness of the new culture, immigrants often quickly realise that assimilating themselves into their new culture is a valuable way to avoid social ostracism and poverty for themselves and their children.

Today, the assimilationist viewpoint is thought to be wrong, and liberalism assumes that we cannot understand freedom without culture, and that caring about the former means respecting and recognising the latter. Indeed, the capacity to make choices and evaluate their values is seen through the lens of culture. Without this filter, individuals would not have the tools needed to value certain practices. Abiding by this perspective, philosopher Will Kymlicka states the following.

> Whether or not a course of action has any significance for us depends on whether, and how, our language renders vivid to us the point of that activity. And the way in which language renders vivid these activities is shaped by our history, our traditions and conventions. Understanding these cultural narratives is a precondition of making intelligent judgements about how to lead our lives. In this sense, our culture not only provides options, it also provides the spectacle through which we identify experiences as valuable (1995, p. 83).

Consequently, Walzer also assumes that death is not only physical but can also be spiritual and leave individuals helpless when the filter through which they are able to make meaningful choices for themselves disappears and is replaced by a totally different cultural blueprint. For him, a political community allows people to understand themselves, and is a source of their individual identity, which is why it must be preserved. On the other hand, replacing it coercively with totally different sets of beliefs is not morally acceptable (2004, pp. 49–50). However, if political communities have the right to survive for the sake of their members' freedom, this means that all human societies, irrespective of what they stand for, have an inherent right to resort to terrorism against an enemy that threatens the survival of their culture and collective values. Readers understand that this logic leads to a major problem. If we are to believe that all cultures matter, this means that the Nazis were justified at the beginning of 1943—what I believe was the turning point of the conflict when it became obvious that Hitler would lose the war—to resort to total war against their enemies that were threatening to eradicate Nazi culture[85]. If we are to believe that the true 'evil' we ought to avoid at all costs—even if it means resorting to terrorism—is the disappearance of a culture irrespective of what constitutes its core values and principles, then we may be forced to agree with the sometimes uncomfortable premise that all cultures—even immoral ones—have the right to defend themselves with all possible means when they believe that it is their enemy's wish to eradicate their community.

Believing in the moral equality of cultures is therefore significantly different from the one that lies in the idea that communities ought to fight with all possible means, even resorting to terrorism, *only* when they are facing an imminent defeat at the hands of a *morally inferior* society. However, this view is held by Walzer in *Just and Unjust Wars* where he links the criterion of facing an imminent defeat with the moral nature of our enemy. What he writes leaves no doubt in this regard:

> That is what I am going to assume, at any rate, on behalf of all those people who believed at the time and still believe a third of a century later that Nazism was an ultimate threat to everything decent in our lives, an ideology and a practice of domination so murderous, so degrading even to those who might survive, that the consequences of its final victory were literally beyond calculation, immeasurably awful. We see it-and I don't use the phrase lightly-as evil objectified in the world, and in a form so potent and apparent that there could never have been anything to do but fight against it. I obviously cannot offer an account of Nazism in these pages. But such an account is hardly necessary. It is enough to point to the historical experience of Nazi rule. Here was a threat to human values so radical that its imminence would surely constitute a supreme emergency (2006, p. 253).

Following this view, we must conclude that resorting to terrorism against the Nazis was justified on the basis that they were threatening to eradicate everything connected with modern notions of freedom and equality in order to replace them with the idea that some races are superior to others and to the absolute submission of individuals to their collectivity: notions that, if the Nazis had prevailed, would have for sure been a moral setback for humanity. This is, therefore,

---

[85] Which was openly claimed by Joseph Goebbels on February 18, 1943.

a basic assumption of Walzer's doctrine of supreme emergency, namely that there are some values and norms that are objectively superior to others.

Consequently, his assumption that some ways of life have more value than others creates a major difficulty in determining when states and societies ought to be excused for rejecting the moral rules of warfare and resorting to terrorism. If the superiority of the values and principles of liberalism over those linked with Nazism is not difficult to establish (well, I can only hope that it is the case for all my readers), it can prove less easy when other types of communities are facing each other. How should we determine whether a supreme emergency ought to exist when a nonliberal society threatens to eradicate the way of life of another nonliberal society? For the sake of this argument, let us imagine that during the 1980–1988 war between Iraq and Iran, Saddam Hussein would have been on the verge of being defeated: a defeat that would have meant the imposition of an Islamic theocracy on the Iraqi people and the end of his secular dictatorship. Would he have been able to claim the right to resort to terrorist tactics against his enemy, on the basis that the Ayatollah-type regime would have constituted a moral setback for his people? How can one determine when one type of non-liberal value has more or less value than another non-liberal way of life? In the absence of clear indicators, we are at risk of having a very subjectively excusing terrorism.

Alternatively, perhaps Walzer's underlying view is that only liberal societies —thought to be the most accomplished form human societies can become—have an inherent right to reject the moral rules of warfare when they are facing a nonliberal foe. If this is the case, then Walzer advocates a similar view of the value of violence as that held by Bertrand Russell, who only saw value in it when it served the overall benefits of mankind (1915)[86]. What this means is that beyond the idea that only liberal states could claim a supreme emergency, this logic that elevates the Western values of liberalism to an ideal other society should aspire to would also contribute to giving weight to the idea that colonisation of nonliberal societies is acceptable, as well as to invalidate the legitimacy of the numerous claims of Aboriginal people living in America and Australia on the basis that the harm their ancestors suffered nonetheless ultimately allowed them to become members of a superior civilisation. Among other things, holding such a view is highly problematic as it tends to shift the focus from fighting 'just wars' in favor of fighting 'moral wars' and to posit a judgmental appraisal of civ-

---

86 According to his view, there are 4 types of wars: 1/ Wars of colonization ; 2/ Wars of principle ; 3/ Wars of self-defence ; and 4/ Wars of prestige. He argues that the first three types of war may be justified insofar as they are led against adversaries of inferior civilization.

ilisations from an ethnocentric perspective. This may have made sense in the 19th century, but it is no longer an acceptable point of view.

Apart from this incoherence in Walzer's theory, I believe that the second most fundamental criticism we can address in his doctrine of supreme emergency lies in how the resort to terroristic means can be justified and how these potential reasons may outweigh the deontological obligation we have not to negotiate absolute moral norms. Walzer claims in this regard that when societies are facing a supreme emergency, they may be justified in ignoring the normal moral limits that people would otherwise choose to respect. When this happens, people will oppose two moral values, *innocence* on the one hand and *preserving the lives of those who are threatened by the immoral actor*, and will most likely come to the conclusion that the latter ought to be privileged over the former. However, the question that needs to be answered is whether ignoring the moral rules of warfare and resorting to terrorism might in any significant way help preserve the lives of those facing imminent defeat of an immoral enemy. If this is not the case, then this utilitarian calculation would simply lose its value, and there are reasons to believe that this is the case.

Indeed, the logic behind resorting to terrorism when facing imminent defeat against a highly immoral enemy is to prevent this foe from achieving total victory. Resorting to indiscriminate actions is in this sense the ultimate last stand against evil as it is understood that after the fall of 'the Alamo', nothing will be able to hinder that criminal entity from eradicating politically and physically its victims. All other justifications are therefore unacceptable, such as wanting revenge for the indiscriminate bombings of our own cities. Of course, forcing the enemy to experience the same reality he is imposing on us may lead us to believe that justice is being served according to Talion Law, but vengeance does not increase our chances of preventing our enemy from conquering us. The same fate awaits the idea that resorting to terrorism will decrease our enemies' chances of success. This assumption is based on the hope that it will demoralise the civilian population and impact their willingness to continue fighting. Unfortunately, this logic simply did not prove itself accurate during WWII with the German population, who, despite seeing its cities burned to the ground, never turned itself against its *Führer*. The reason for this may simply be in authoritarian or totalitarian regimes (which are probably the most likely to threaten the core values of humanity); citizens face tremendously harsh consequences for their dissidence and resistance, which is why they usually suffer in silence. Furthermore, with the help of state propaganda, the resort to indiscriminate means of warfare or alternatives to war on the part of their enemies may simply boost their morale and lead them to rally around their flag and to support those who are ruling their state, thereby creating a situation that does not increase the victim's chances to prevent the immoral enemy from winning. A good example at the moment is Putin's Russia which has faced the most extreme set of economic sanctions ever imposed against a state. While some measures specifically target key people of the regime who have engaged their moral responsibility in the unlawful decision to invade Ukraine, many of them will nonetheless end up having highly indiscriminate impacts on Russian civilians whose innocence has not been challenged by their president's decision to launch a war of aggression (Caron, 2022e). However, this has not negatively impacted their support for Vladimir Putin, which has seen a significant rise according to the Levada Centre, the only independent polling research organisation in Russia[87]. Moreover, the focus on the indiscriminate targeting of one's enemy comes at the expense of what actually makes the biggest difference in our capacity to prevent him from conquering us, namely, prioritising the targeting of military infrastructures and facilities. While we are spending efforts and resources on bombing cities that may have no military significance at all, our immoral enemy, against whom we are facing an imminent defeat, has the luxury of building more planes and tanks in its factories and mobilising even more troops against us. From a military perspective, this approach is counterproductive and hinders what ought to be the fundamental reason behind resorting to terroristic means. In this sense, it is difficult to see how resorting to terrorism in exceptional circumstances could ever be justified.

In conclusion, when it comes to justifying terrorism in exceptional circumstances, I believe that the dangers of trying to escape from an absolutist view of rights, that is, the belief in the absolute inviolability of certain moral rules, are too high and lie on highly questionable premises. For the reasons I have discussed in the second part of this chapter, trying to excuse terrorism is no more than opening a Pandora's box that would liberate a utilitarian logic that would quickly lead to a validation of widespread violence under the excuse that the end justifies the means to transform our current view of war into an Augustinian understanding that one's moral superiority is the only needed justification to harm and kill other human beings. As such, terrorism (as I have defined it) remains in my mind a type of violence that can never be justified.

---

[87] https://www.levada.ru/en/2022/04/11/approval-of-institutions-ratings-of-parties-and-politicians/

Conclusion

Defining terrorism as the deliberate targeting of innocent people has many advantages. One of them is its ability to offer a distinctive view of what this type of political violence refers to, as well as making a necessary conceptual clarification with its 'little cousin', guerrilla warfare. Although they share some common features, these two concepts cannot be used interchangeably as if they were synonymous. If terrorism can never be justified, even to achieve a noble objective, the same cannot be said with guerrilla when some specific contextual criteria are met. When the conditions described in this book are satisfied, guerrilla actions can be deemed necessary and not inherently immoral, as those targeted by them cannot be considered innocent. If a spirit of nobility can be attributed to guerrilla, the same is impossible with terrorism that remains inherently connected with barbarianism and immorality. But making such distinctions are impossible when terrorism is thought as a catch-all term.

Furthermore, the definition of terrorism I have privileged also allows us to have a better idea of the various ethical dilemmas it raises, more specifically, those associated with states' obligation to ensure safety to their own citizens. Further, these dilemmas should not be minimised as one of them (discussed in chapter 3) has led to one of the most immoral and strategic miscalculation of warfare history, that is the so-called 'war on terror' fought largely, but not exclusively, by the United States. Considering the tragic consequences this war had on millions of innocent people worldwide, it is clear to any objective observer that Western states have engaged themselves on a wrong path as if facing this type of threat constituted some sort of a blank check regarding the actions state entities are allowed to undertake to eliminate that menace. Needless to say that this is an inappropriate perspective. Yes, terrorism might be an immoral form of political violence, but evil should never be fought with evil. Being able to find a proper balance between security and defence is not an easy task, and requires imagination. Any misjudgment in this regard may easily lead states fighting terrorism to become terroristic entities, which can never be permitted.

https://doi.org/10.1515/9783110757569-007

Bibliography

Allhoff, Fritz (2011). "Torture Warrants, Self-Defense, and Necessity", *Public Affairs Quarterly*, Vol. 25, No. 3, pp. 217–240.

Annan, Kofi (2005). *Kofi Annan's keynote address to the closing plenary of the International Summit on Democracy, Terrorism and Security*, United Nations, March 10. Available at: https://www.un.org/sg/en/content/sg/speeches/2005-03-10/kofi-annan's-keynote-ad dress-closing-plenary-international-summit

Arendt, Hannah (1958). *The Origins of Totalitarianism*. Cleveland: World.

Augustine. *The City of God*.

Bellamy, Alex (2006). "No Pain, No Gain? Torture and Ethics in the War on Terror", *International Affairs*, Vol. 82, No. 1, pp. 121–148.

Bernstein, Richard (2003). "Kidnapping Has Germans Debating Police Torture", *The New York Times*, April 10.

Bessner, Daniel and Michael Stauch (2010). "Karl Heinzen and the Intellectual Origins of Modern Terror", *Terrorism and Political Violence*, Vol. 22, No. 2, pp. 143–176.

Bethke Elshtain, Jean. (2006). "Jean Bethke Elshtain Responds", *Dissent*, Summer, pp. 109–111.

Bethke Elshtain, Jean. (2013). "Prevention, preemption, and other conundrums", in Deen K. Chatterjee (ed.), *The Ethics of Preventive War*. Cambridge: Cambridge University Press, pp. 15–26.

Bin Laden, Osama (2005). *Messages to the World: The Statements of Osama Bin Laden*. London: Verso.

Bonner, Raymond, Don van Natta Jr and Amy Waldman (2003). "Threats and Responses Interrogations; Questioning Suspects In a Dark and Surreal World", *New York Times*, March 9. Available at: https://www.nytimes.com/2003/03/09/world/threats-responses-in terrogations-questioning-terror-suspects-dark-surreal-world.html

Branche, Raphaëlle (2001). *La torture et l'armée pendant la guerre d'Algérie: 1954–1962*. Paris: Gallimard.

Bump, Philip (2018). "15 years after the Iraq War began, the death toll is still murky", *The Washington Post*, March 20. Available at:https://www.washingtonpost.com/news/poli tics/wp/2018/03/20/15-years-after-it-began-the-death-toll-from-the-iraq-war-is-still-murky/

Buzar, Stipe (2020). "The Principle of Double Effect and Just War Theory", *Philosophia*, Vol. 48, No. 4, pp. 1299–1312.

Byman, Daniel L. (2009). "Do Targeted Killings Work?", The Brookings Institute, July. Available at: https://www.brookings.edu/opinions/do-targeted-killings-work-2/

Camus, Albert (1958). "The Just Assassins," in *Caligula and Three Other Plays*, Translated by Stuart Gilbert. New York: Alfred A. Knopf.

Canto-Sperber, Monique (2010). *L'idée de guerre juste*. Paris: PUF.

Caron, Jean-François (2012). "Rooted Cosmopolitanism in Canada and Quebec's National Identities", *National Identities*, Vol. 14, No. 2, pp. 351–366.

Caron, Jean-François (2014). "An Ethical and Judicial Framework for Mercy Killing on the Battlefield", *Journal of Military Ethics*, Vol. 13, No. 3, pp. 228–239.

Caron, Jean-François (2015). *La guerre juste: les enjeux éthiques de la guerre au 21ème siècle*. Québec: Les Presses de l'Université Laval.

https://doi.org/10.1515/9783110757569-008

Caron, Jean-François (2018). *Disobedience in the Military: Legal and Ethical Implications.* Singapore: Springer.

Caron, Jean-François (2019a). "On Human Nature and How to Control it", in *The Prince 2.0: Applying Machiavellian Strategy to Contemporary Political Life.* Singapore: Springer, pp. 23 – 32.

Caron, Jean-François (2019b). "On the Objectives of Governments: Preventing Domestic Conflicts", in *The Prince 2.0: Applying Machiavellian Strategy to Contemporary Political Life.* Singapore: Springer, pp. 13 – 22.

Caron, Jean-François (2019c). "When it is Necessary to Entrust Governance to One Individual: To Save a Democracy and Its Principles", in *The Prince 2.0: Applying Machiavellian Strategy to Contemporary Political Life.* Singapore: Springer, pp. 39 – 44.

Caron, Jean-François (2019d). "The Necessity to Entrust Power to One Individual: To Create a New State", in *The Prince 2.0: Applying Machiavellian Strategy to Contemporary Political Life.* Singapore: Springer, pp. 45 – 54.

Caron, Jean-François (2019e). *Contemporary Technologies and the Morality of Warfare: The War of the Machines.* London: Routledge.

Caron, Jean-François (2019f). "Exploring the Extent of Ethical Disobedience Through the Lens of the Srebrenica and Rwanda Genocides: Can Soldiers Disobey Lawful Orders?", *Critical Military Studies*, Vol. 5, No. 1, 2019, pp. 1 – 20.

Caron, Jean-François (2020a). "Defining semi-autonomous, automated and autonomous weapon systems in order to understand their ethical challenges", *Digital War*, Vol. 1, No. 1 – 3, pp. 173 – 177. Available at: https://link.springer.com/article/10.1057/s42984-020-00028-5.

Caron, Jean-François (2020b). *A Sketch of the World After the Covid-19 Crisis: Essays on Political Authority, The Future of Globalization and the Rise of China.* Singapore: Springer.

Caron, Jean-François (2021a). *Violent Alternatives to War: Justifying Actions Against Contemporary Terrorism.* Berlin: De Gruyter.

Caron, Jean-François (2021b). *Irresponsible Citizenship: The Cultural Roots of the Crisis of Authority in Times of Pandemic.* New York: Peter Lang.

Caron, Jean-François (2021c). *La citoyenneté irresponsable: Les racines culturelles de la crise de l'autorité en temps de pandémie.* Québec: Presses de l'Université Laval

Caron, Jean-François (2021d). "The Ties that Bind: Kymlicka and the Problem of Political Unity in Multination States", *Border and Regional Studies*, Vol. 9, No. 3, pp. 105 – 127.

Caron, Jean-François and Viktoriya Malikova (2021). "Understanding Anti-Regime Activist' Failures During the 2019 Kazakhstan Presidential Election", in Jean-François Caron (ed.) *Understanding Kazakhstan's 2019 Political Transition.* Singapore: Springer, pp. 79 – 100.

Caron, Jean-François (2022a). *The Great Lockdown: Western Societies and the Fear of Death.* New York: Peter Lang.

Caron, Jean-François (2022b). *Le grand confinement: L'Occident et la peur de la mort.* Québec: Presses de l'Université Laval.

Caron, Jean-François (2022c). *Marginalisé. Réflexions sur l'isolement du Canada dans les relations internationales.* Québec: Presses de l'Université Laval.

Caron, Jean-François (2022d). "Terrorism and the Lawful Preemptive Use of Force: The Case of Cyberattacks", *Digital War*. Available at: https://link.springer.com/article/10.1057/s42984-022-00043-8

Caron, Jean-François (2022e). "Des sanctions économiques immorales", *Institute for Peace and Diplomacy.* Avilable at: https://nur.nu.edu.kz/bitstream/handle/123456789/6112/Des-sanctions-economiques-immorales.pdf?sequence=1&isAllowed=y

Carter, David B. (2016). "Provocation and the Strategy of Terrorist and Guerrilla Attacks", *International Organizations*, Vol. 70, No. 1, pp. 133–173.

Chaliand, Gérard and Arnaud Blin (2015). *Histoire du terrorisme: De l'Antiquité à Daesh.* Paris: Fayard.

Chamayou, Grégoire (2015). *A Theory of the Drone.* New York: The New Press.

Chatterjee, Deen K. (2013). *The Ethics of Preventive War.* Cambridge: Cambridge University Press.

Cigar, Norman (2009). *Al-Qa'Ida's Doctrine For Insurgency: Abd Al-'Aziz Al-Muqrin's A Practical Course for Guerrilla War.* Lincoln: Potomac Book.

Coady, C.A.J. (1985). "The Morality of Terrorism", *Philosophy*, Vol. 60, No. 231, pp. 47–69.

Cook, Martin L. (2007). "Michael Walzer's Concept of 'Supreme Emergency'", *Journal of Military Ethics*, Vol. 6, No. 2, pp. 138–151.

Cronin, Audrey Kurth (2002/2003). "Behind the Curve: Globalization and International Terrorism", *International Security*, Vol. 27, No. 3, pp. 30–58.

De Vattel, Emir (2008). *The Law of Nations.* Indianapolis: Liberty Fund.

Dershowitz, Alan (2002). *Why Terrorism Works: Understanding the Threat, Responding to the Challenge.* New Haven: Yale University Press.

Dershowitz, Alan (2004). "The torture Warrant: A Response to Professor Strauss", *NYLS Law Review*, Vol. 48, No. 1, pp. 275–294.

Dipert, Randall R. (2006). "Preventive War and the Epistemological Dimension of the Morality of War", *Journal of Military Ethics*, Vol. 5, No. 1, pp. 32–54.

Draper, Kai (1998). "Self-Defence, Collective Obligation, and Noncombatant Liability", *Social Theory and Practice*, Vol. 24, No. 1, pp. 57–81.

English, Richard (2003). *Armed Struggle: The History of the IRA.* London: Palgrave MacMillan.

Feinberg, Joel (1970). *Doing & Deserving: Essays in the Theory of Responsibility.* Princeton: Princeton University Press.

Finlay, Christopher (2015). *Terrorism and the Right to Resist: A Theory of Just Revolutionary War.* Cambridge: Cambridge University Press.

Fletcher, George (1998). *Basic Concepts of Criminal Law.* Oxford: Oxford University Press.

Friedrich, Carl and Zbigniew Brzezinski (1965). *Totalitarian Dictatorship and Autocracy.* Cambridge, Mass: Harvard University Press.

Gartzke, Eric (2013). "The Myth of Cyberwar: Bringing War in Cyberspace Back Down to Earth", *International Security*, Vol. 38, No. 2, pp. 41–73.

Gazette des Tribunaux. April 29, 1894, pp. 417–419.

Gert, Bernard (1969). "Justifying Violence", *The Journal of Philosophy*, Vol. 66, No. 19, pp. 616–628.

Granhag, Pär Anders, Steven M. Kleinman and Simon Oleszkiewicz (2016). "The Scharff Technique: On How to Effectively Elicit Intelligence from Human Sources", *International Journal of Intelligence and Counterintelligence*, Vol. 29, No. 1, pp. 132–150.

Gross, Michael (2015). *The Ethics of Insurgency: A Critical Guide to Just Guerrilla Warfare.* Cambridge: Cambridge University Press.

Gross, Michael and Tamar Meisels (eds.) (2017). *Soft War: The Ethics of Unarmed Conflict.* Cambridge: Cambridge University Press.

Grotius, Hugo. *De Jure Belli ac Pacis.*

Guevara, Ernesto (2007). *Guerrilla Warfare.* Hawthorn: BN Publishing.

Hoffman, Bruce (1993). "'Holy Terror': the Implications of Terrorism Motivated by a Religious Imperative", *RAND Paper.* Available at:https://www.rand.org/pubs/papers/P7834.html

Hopkinson, Michael (2004). *The Irish War of Independence.* Dublin: Gill & MacMillan.

Handbook for Volunteers of the Irish Republican Army. Notes on Guerrilla Warfare. (1956).

Holmes, Robert L. (1989). *On War and Morality.* Princeton, NJ: Princeton University Press.

Ingram, Haroro J., Craig Whiteside and Charlie Winter (2020). *The ISIS Reader: Milestone Texts of the Islamic State Movement.* London: Hurts & Company.

International Court of Justice (1986). *Nicaragua v. United States.* Available at:https://www.icj-cij.org/public/files/case-related/70/070-19860627-JUD-01-00-EN.pdf https://www.icj-cij.org/public/files/case-related/70/070-19860627-JUD-01-00-EN.pdf

Jaspers, Karl (2000). *The Question of German Guilt.* New York: Fordham University Press.

Kymlicka, Will (1995). *Multicultural Citizenship. A Liberal Theory of Minority Rights.* Oxford: Oxford University Press.

Laqueur, Walter (2004). *Voices of Terror: Manifestos, Writings and Manuals of Al Qaeda, Hamas, and Other Terrorists From Around the World and Throughout the Ages.* Naperville, Illinois: Sourcebooks.

Laqueur, Walter (2017). *A History of Terrorism: Expanded Edition.* London & New York: Routledge.

Laqueur, Walter and Christopher Wall (2018). *The Future of Terrorism: ISIS, Al-Qaeda, and the Alt-Right.* New York: St. Martin's Press.

Lee, Steven (2004). "Double Effect, Double Intention, And Asymmetric Warfare", *Journal of Military Ethics*, Vol. 3, No. 3, pp. 233–251.

Luban, David (2004). "Preventive War", *Philosophy and Public Affairs*, Vol. 32, No. 3, pp. 207–248.

Luban, David (2007). "Preventive War and Human Rights", in Henry Shue and David Rodin (eds.), *Preemption: Military Action and Moral Justification.* Oxford: Oxford University Press, pp. 171–201.

Lund, William R. (2011). "Reconsidering Supreme Emergencies: Michael Walzer and his Critics", *Social Theory and Practice*, Vol. 37 No. 4, pp. 654–678.

MacMaster, Neil (2004). "Torture: From Algiers to Abu Ghraib", *Race and Class*, Vol. 46, No. 2, pp. 1–21.

Maizland, Lindsay (2022). "A Look at Afghanistan's Humanitarian Crisis", Council on Foreign Relations. Available at: https://www.cfr.org/article/afghanistan-humanitarian-crisis-famine-foreign-aid-taliban

Malanczuk, Peter (1991). "The Kurdish Crisis and Allied Intervention in the Aftermath of the Second Gulf War", *European Journal of International Law*, Vol. 2, No. 2, pp. 114–132.

Manulak, Daniel (2020). "'A marathon, not a sprint': Canada and South African Apartheid, 1987–1990", *International Journal*, Vol. 75, No. 1, pp. 83–94.

Marighella, Carlos (1969). *Minimanual of the Urban Guerrilla.* Available at: https://www.marxists.org/archive/marighella-carlos/1969/06/minimanual-urban-guerrilla/

McAdam, Doug, Sidney Tarrow and Charles Tilly (2001). *Dynamics of Contention.* Cambridge: Cambridge University Press.

McMahan, Jeff (2004). "The Ethics of Killing in War", *Ethics*, Vol. 114, July, pp. 693–733.

McPherson Lionel K. (2004). "Innocence and Responsibility in War", *Canadian Journal of Philosophy*, Vol. 34, No. 4, pp. 485–506.

Metraux, Daniel A. (1995). "Religious Terrorism in Japan: The Fatal Appeal of Aum Shinrikyo", *Asian Survey*, Vol. 35, No. 12, pp. 1140–1154.

Miller, Seumas (2009). *Terrorism and Counter-Terrorism: Ethics and Liberal Democracy*. Oxford: Blackwell.

Narveson, Jan (1965). "Pacifism: A Philosophical Analysis ", *Ethics*, Vol. 75, No. 4, pp. 259–271.

Nathanson, Stephen (2010). *Terrorism and the Ethics of War*. Cambridge: Cambridge University Press.

Neff, Stephen C. (2005). *War and the Law of Nations: A General History*. Cambridge: Cambridge University Press.

Neu, Michael (2013). "The Supreme Emergency of War: A Critique of Walzer", *Journal of International Political Theory*, Vol. 10, No. 1, pp. 3–19.

Neumann, Peter R. (2009). *Old and New Terrorism*. Cambridge: Polity.

Nicholls, Steven (2007). "Terrorism, Millenarianism, and death: A Study of Hezbollah and Aum Shinrikyo", Edith Cowan University. Available at: https://ro.ecu.edu.au/cgi/view content.cgi?article=2294&context=theses_hons

O'Mara, Shane (2015). *Why torture Doesn't Work: The Neuroscience of Interrogation*. Cambridge, Mass: Harvard University Press.

O'Neill, Bard E. (2005). *Insurgency & Terrorism: From Revolution to Apocalypse*. Lincoln: Potomac Book.

Orend, Brian (2013). *The Morality of War*. 2nd edn. Toronto: Broadview Press.

Pattison, James (2018). *The Alternatives to War: From Sanctions to Nonviolence*. Oxford: Oxford University Press.

Pellissier, Pierre (1995). *La Bataille d'Alger*. Paris: Perrin.

Polk, William R. (2008). *Violent Politics: A History of Insurgency, Terrorism & Guerrilla War, From the American Revolution to Iraq*. New York: Harper Collins.

Powers, Thomas (1995). "Was it Right?", *The Atlantic*, July. Available at: https://www.the atlantic.com/magazine/archive/1995/07/was-it-right/376364/

Predelli, Stefano (2004). "Bombers: Some Comments on Double Effects and Harmful Involvement", *Journal of Military Ethics*, Vol. 3, No. 1, pp. 16–26.

Primoratz, Igor (2013). *Terrorism: A Philosophical Investigation*. Cambridge, UK: Polity Press.

Radsan, Rafsheen John (2005). "The Moussaoui Case: The Mess from Minnesota", *William Mitchell Law Review*, Vol. 31, No. 4, pp. 1417–1459.

Rapoport, David C. (1984). "Fear and Trembling: Terrorism in Three Religious Traditions", *American Political Science Review*, Vol. 78, No. 3, pp. 658–677.

Reike, Ruben (2012). "Libya and the Responsibility to Protect: Lessons for the Prevention of Mass Atrocities", *St Anthony's International Review*, Vol. 8, No. 1, pp. 122–149.

Rejali, Darius (2007). *Torture and Democracy*. Princeton: Princeton University Press.

Risse, Thomas (2000). "Let's Argue! Communicative Action in World Politics", *International Organization*, Vol. 54, No. 1, pp. 1–39.

Russell, Bertrand (1915). "The Ethics of War", *The International Journal of Ethics*, Vol. 25, No. 2, pp. 127–142.

Schmid, Alex P. (1992). "The Response Problem as a Definition Problem", *Terrorism and Political Violence*, Vol. 4, No. 4, pp. 7–13.

Schweller, Randall L. (1992). "Domestic Structure and Preventive War: Are Democracies More Pacific?", *World Politics*, Vol. 44, No. 2, pp. 235–269.

Shock, Kurt (1999). "People Power and Political Opportunities: Social Movement Mobilization and Outcomes in the Philippines and Burma", *Social Problems*, Vol. 46, No. 3, pp. 355–375.

Sedgwick, Mark (2004). "Al-Qaeda and the Nature of Religious Terrorism", *Terrorism and Political Violence*, Vol. 16, No. 4, pp. 795–814.

Shaw, Martin (2005). *The New Western Way of War*. Cambridge: Polity Press.

Shimoda et al. v. the State (1963). District Court, Tokyo Japan. Available at: https://www. asser.nl/upload/documents/DomCLIC/Docs/NLP/Japan/Shimoda_TokyoDistrictCourt_7-12-1963.pdf

Shue, Henry (1996). *Basic Rights: Subsistence, Affluence, and US Foreign Policy*. 2nd edn. Princeton: Princeton University Press.

Simon, Steven and Daniel Benjamin (2000). "America and the New Terrorism", *Survival*, Vol. 42, No. 1, pp. 59–75.

Singer, David J. and Mel Small (1972). *The Wages of War, 1816–1965: A Statistical Handbook*. New York: Wiley.

Stern, Menahem (n.d.). "Zealots and Sicarii", *Encyclopaedia Judaica*, Encyclopedia.com. Available at: https://www.encyclopedia.com/religion/encyclopedias-almanacs-tran scripts-and-maps/zealots-and-sicarii (accessed August 22, 2022).

Strehle, Stephen (2004). "Saddam Hussein, Islam, and Just War Theory: The Case for a Pre-emptive Strike", *Political Theology*, Vol. 5, No. 1, pp. 76–101

Sussman, David (2005). "What's Wrong with Torture?", *Philosophy & Public Affairs*, Vol. 33, No. 1, pp. 1–33.

Taylor Wilkins, Burleigh (1992). *Terrorism and Collective Responsibility*. London: Routledge.

Thompson, Allan (ed.) (2007). *The Medias and the Rwanda Genocide*. Ann Arbor: Pluto Press.

Thornton, T. P. (1964). "Terror as a Weapon of Political Agitation", in Harry Eckstein (ed.), *Iternal War: Poroblems and Approaches*. New York: Free Press, pp. 71–99.

Tindale, Christopher (1996). "The Logic of Torture: A Critical Examination", *Social Theory and Practice*, Vol. 22, No. 3, pp. 349–374.

Tinker, Jerry M. (1971). "The Political Power of Non-Violent Resistance: The Gandhian Technique", *The Western Political Quarterly*, Vol. 24, No. 4, pp. 775–788.

Toner, Christopher (2005). "Just War and the Supreme Emergency Exemption", *The Philosophical Quarterly*, Vol. 55, No. 221, pp. 545–561.

Walzer, Michael (1973). "Political Action: The Problem of Dirty Hands", *Philosophy & Public Affairs*, Vol. 2, No. 2, pp. 160–180.

Walzer, Michael (2004). *Arguing About War*. New Haven & London: Yale University Press.

Walzer, Michael (2006). *Just and Unjust Wars: A Moral Argument with Historical Illustrations*. 4th edn. New York: Basic Books.

Warren Smith, J. (2007). "Augustine and the Limits of Preemptive and Preventive War", *Journal of Religious Ethics*, Vol. 35, No. 1, pp. 141–162.

Watson Institute for International & Public Affairs, Brown University. (2020). "Afghan Civilians", *Costs of War*. Available at: https://watson.brown.edu/costsofwar/costs/human/civilians/afghan (last updated August 2022).

Wellmann, Carl (1979). "On Terrorism Itself", *Journal of Value Inquiry*, Vol. 13, pp. 250–258.

Wolfendale, Jessica (2017). "Defining War", in Michael L. Gross and Tamar Meisels (eds.), *Soft War: The Ethics of Unarmed Conflict*. Cambridge: Cambridge University Press, pp. 16–32.

Xenophon. *Anabasis*.

Index

https://doi.org/10.1515/9783110757569-009

www.ingramcontent.com/pod-product-compliance
Lightning Source LLC
Chambersburg PA
CBHW021623270326
41931CB00008B/838